Imamate

Shahīd Ayatullāh Murtadhā
Mutahharī

AL-BURĀQ
Heighten The Mind

Copyright

ISBN: 978-1-956276-08-4 (Paperback).

Translated and annotated by al-Burāq Publications. Where needed, context and transliterations were added.

Printed and published by al-Burāq Publications.

Ordering Information
We offer discounts and promotions for wholesale purchases and for non-profit organizations, libraries, and other educational institutions. Contact us at the email below for further information.

www.al-Buraq.org
publications@al-Buraq.org

First printed edition | November 2021

Dedication

The publication of this book was made possible through the generous support of our donors.

Please recite *Sūrah al-Fātiha* and ask Allāh for the Divine reward (*thawāb*) to be conferred upon the donors and also the souls of all the deceased in whose memory their loved ones have contributed graciously towards the publication of *Imamate.*

We want to begin by giving all praise and thanks to Allah ﷻ for giving us the tawfiq to translate this book. He has guided us and without Him, we would not have been guided to the straight path embodied by the Prophet Muhammad ﷺ and the Ahl al-Bayt ؑ.

This book is dedicated firstly to Shahīd Ayatullāh Murťadhā Muťahharī, who made tremendous strides in advancing the cause of Islam. It is also dedicated to all the scholars, martyrs and believers who worked tirelessly to promote the pure Muhammadan path.

We want to also give our thanks and appreciation to all believers from around the world and acknowledge the team which helped al-Burāq Publications complete this work, spending countless hours to make its publication possible. Please recite Sūrah al-Fātiḥah on behalf of them and their marhūmēn .

This book is dedicated in honor of the following individuals. Please remember them in your prayers and may Allah ﷻ have mercy on them and their loved ones.

Abdo Hamad Nasser-eddine

Abdul Hussen Amin Saad

Ali Ahmed Ftouni

Ali Baydoun

Ali Tazarvi

Alya Victoria Agemy Yazback

Amatul Fatima Razvi

Bande Khuda

Georgi Abass Talevski

Haidar Alaouie

Hajah Al-Mustrah

Hajj Ahmad Mahmoud Ghamlouche

Hajj Ali Hammoud

Hajj Ali Youssef Amin Dabaja

Hajj Deeb H. Aoun

Hajj Hassan Mahmoud Sobh

Hajj Hussein Ali Aoun

Hajj Youssef Joey Ali Chami

Hajjeh Souad Bitar

Hajji Amneh Mahmoud Sobh-Ftouni

Hajji Iman Elsaghir

Hajji Mariam Serhan

Hassan Khalil Beydoun

Hussein Khalil

Mahmoud Tiba

Mehrunnisa Shariff

Mohammad Jassem Al-Rubaie

Mohammed Hasan Naqvi

Munawwar Jehan

Munib Baydoun

Najibeh Baydoun

Nazih Kassem Baydoun

Radhiya Alqallaf

Ramzanali ValiMohammed

Shaheed Sayed Khaled
Mahmoud Abdallah Saleh

Shandar Fatima

Syed Jaffar Hussain

Syed Mehdi Hussain Rizvi

Syed Nawab Raza Kazmi

Turfah Kassem Sobh

Zeinab Baydoun

Terms of Respect

The following Arabic phrases have been used throughout this book in their respective places to show the reverence which the noble personalities deserve.

عزّ وجلّ

Used for Allāh (God) meaning:
Exalted and Sublime (Perfect) is He

صلى الله عليه وآله وسلم

Used for Prophet Muḥammad meaning:
Blessings from Allāh be upon him and his family

عليه السلام

Used for a man of high status (singular) meaning:
Peace be upon him

عليها السلام

Used for woman of a high status (singular) meaning:
Peace be upon her

عليهما السلام

Used for men/women of a high status (dual) meaning:
Peace be upon them both

عليهم السلام

Used for men and/or women of a high status (plural) meaning:
Peace be upon them all

قدس سره

Used for a deceased scholar meaning:
May his resting [burial] place remain pure

Duaa al-Huja

اللهم كن لوليك الحجة بن الحسن صلواتك
عليه وعلى آبائه في هذه الساعة وفي كل
ساعة وليا وحافظا وقائدا وناصرا ودليلا
وعينا حتى تسكنه أرضك طوعا وتمتعه فيها طويلا

O Allah, be, for Your representative, the Hujjat (proof), son of al-Hasan, Your blessings be upon him and his forefathers, in this hour and in every hour: a guardian, a protector, a leader, a helper, a proof, and an eye - until You make him live on the Earth, in obedience (to You), and cause him to live in it for a long time.

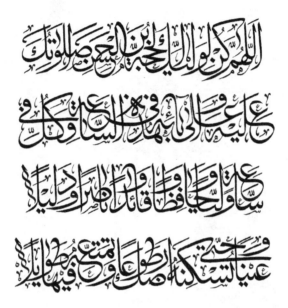

Transliteration Table

The method of transliteration of Islamic terminology from the Arabic language has been carried out according to the standard transliteration table below.

ء	ʾ	ر	r	ف	f
ا	a	ز	z	ق	q
ب	b	س	s	ك	k
ت	t	ش	sh	ل	l
ث	th	ص	ṣ	م	m
ج	j	ض	ḍ	ن	n
ح	ḥ	ط	ṭ	و	w
خ	kh	ظ	ẓ	هـ	h
د	d	ع	ʿ	ي	y
ذ	dh	غ	gh		
Long Vowels					
ا	ā	و	ū	ي	ī
Short Vowels					
ـَ	a	ـُ	u	ـِ	i

Table of Contents

About the Author

Biography of the late Shahīd Ayatullāh Murťadhā Muťahharī

Shahīd Ayatullāh Murťadhā Muťahharī, one of the principle architects of the new Islāmic consciousness in Iran, was born on February 2nd, 1920, in Farīmān, then a village and now a township about sixty kilometres from Mashhad, the great centre of Shī`a pilgrimage and learning in Eastern Iran.

His father was Muhammad Ĥusaīn Muťahharī, a renown scholar who studied in Najaf and spent several years in Egypt and the Hijāz before returning to Farīmān. The elder Muťahharī was of a different caste of mind then his son, who in any event came to outshine him.

Nonetheless, Shahīd Muťahharī always retained great respect and affection for his father, who was also his first teacher.

At the exceptionally early age of twelve, Shahīd Muťahharī began his formal religious studies at the teaching institution in Mashhad, which was then in a state of decline, partly because of internal reasons and partly because of the repressive measures directed by Ridhā Khān, the first Pahlavī autocrat, against all Islāmic institutions.

But in Mashhad, Shahīd Muťahharī discovered his great love for philosophy, theology, and mysticism, a love that remained with him throughout his life and came to shape his entire outlook on religion.

Accordingly, the figure in Mashhad who aroused the greatest devotion in Shahīd Muťahharī was Mīrzā Mahdī Shahīdī Razavī, a teacher of philosophy.

But Razavī died in 1936, before Shahīd Muťahharī was old enough to participate in his classes, and partly because of this reason he left Mashhad the following year to join the growing number of students congregating in the teaching institution in Qum.

Thanks to the skillful stewardship of Shaykh `Abdul Karīm Hā'irī, Qum was on its way to becoming the spiritual and intellectual capital of Islāmic Iran, and Shahīd Muťahharī was able to benefit there from the instruction of a wide range of scholars.

He studied Fiqh and Uŝūl - the core subjects of the traditional curriculum - with Āyatullāh Ĥujjat Kuhkamarī, Āyatullāh Sayyid Muhammad Dāmād, Āyatullāh Sayyid Muhammad Ridhā Gulpāyagānī, and Ĥajj Sayyid Ŝadr al-Dīn as-Ŝadr. But more important than all these was Āyatullāh Burujerdī, the successor of Ĥā'irī as director of the teaching establishment in Qum. Shahīd Muťahharī attended his lectures from his arrival in Qum in 1944 until his departure for Tehran in 1952, and he nourished a deep respect for him.

Fervent devotion and close affinity characterized Shahīd Muťahharī's relationship with his prime mentor in Qum, Imām Khomeinī. When Shahīd Muťahharī arrived in Qum, Imām Khomeinī was a young lecturer, but he was already marked out from his contemporaries by the profoundness and comprehensiveness of his Islāmic vision and his ability to convey it to others.

In about 1946, Imām Khomeinī began lecturing to a small group of students that included both Shahīd Muťahharī and his roommate at the Fayziya Madressah, Āyatullāh Muntazarī, on two key philosophical texts, the Asfar al-Arba`a of Mullā Ŝadra and the Sharh-e-Manzuma of Mullā Hādī Sabzwārī. Shahīd Muťahharī's participation in this group, which continued to meet until about 1951, enabled him to establish more intimate links with his teacher.

In the first two post-war decades, Imām Khomeinī trained numerous students in Qum who became leaders of the Islāmic Revolution and the Islāmic Republic, such that through them (as well as directly), the imprint of his personality was visible on all the key developments of the past decade.

But none among his students bore to Imām Khomeinī the same relationship of affinity as Shahīd Mut'ahharī, an affinity to which the Imām Khomeinī himself has borne witness to.

Among the other teachers whose influence Shahīd Mut'ahharī was exposed to in Qum, was the great exegete of the Qur'ān and philosopher, Āyatullāh Sayyid Muhammad Ĥusain Ťabā'ťabā'ī.

In 1952, Shahīd Mut'ahharī left Qum for Tehran, where he married the daughter of Āyatullāh Rūhānī and began teaching philosophy at the Madrassah Marwi, one of the principal institutions of religious learning in the capital.

In Tehran, Shahīd Mut'ahharī found a broader and more satisfying field of religious, educational, and ultimately political activity. In 1954, he was invited to teach philosophy at the Faculty of Theology and Islāmic Sciences of Tehran University, where he taught for twenty-two years.

A far more important venture in 1965 of the same kind was the foundation of the Ĥusayniya-e-Irshād, an institution in north Tehran, designed to gain the allegiance of the secularly educated young to Islām. Shahīd Mut'ahharī was among the members of the directing board; he also lectured at the Ĥusayniya-e-Irshād and edited and contributed to several of its publications.

In this area, Shahīd Muťahharī's contribution was unique in its volume and scope. Shahīd Muťahharī wrote assiduously and continuously, from his student days in Qum up to 1979, the year of his martyrdom.

When the Islāmic Revolution approached its triumphant climax in the winter of 1978 and Imām Khomeinī left Najaf for Paris, Shahīd Muťahharī was among those who travelled to Paris to meet and consult with him. His closeness to Imām Khomeinī was confirmed by his appointment to the Council of the Islāmic Revolution, the existence of which Imām Khomeinī announced on January 12th, 1979.

Shahīd Muťahharī's services to the Islāmic Revolution were brutally curtailed by his assassination on May 1st, 1979. The murder was carried out by a group known as Furqān, which claimed to be the protagonists of a "progressive Islām," one freed from the allegedly distorting influence of the religious scholars.

Imām Khomeinī wept openly when Shahīd Muťahharī was buried in Qum, and he described him as his "dear son," and as "the fruit of my life," and as "a part of my flesh."

The personage and legacy of Shahīd Muťahharī have certainly remained unforgotten in the Islāmic Republic, to such a degree that his posthumous presence has been almost as impressive as the attainments of his life. The anniversary of his martyrdom is regularly commemorated, and his portrait is ubiquitous throughout Iran.

Many of his unpublished writings are being printed for the first time, and the whole corpus of his work is now being distributed and studied on a massive scale. In the words of Imām Khamene'ī, The Supreme Leader, the works of Shahīd Muṭahharī have come to constitute "the intellectual infrastructure of the Islāmic Republic."

بسم الله الرحمن الرحيم

Arabic Translator's Preface

In the Name of Allāh, the Most Gracious, the Most Merciful

Shahīd Murtaḍā Muṭahharī engaged in a comprehensive approach to provide the basis for doctrinal principles. His approach followed the familiar form used in the domain of the principles of religion: he studied monotheism in a separate volume, followed by a second book on divine justice, a third on prophethood, a fourth on the Imamate and a fifth on the Day of Return. In fact, the doctrinal writings of Shahīd Muṭahharī are not limited to the previously-mentioned books; he also covered other doctrinal topics such as Imām al-Mahdī عجل الله تعالى فرجه الشريف, guardianship, fate, and other principles of faith and doctrine. Anyone who goes back to Shahīd Muṭahharī's doctrinal writings will be attracted by the methodological foundations he sets. The first thing Shahīd Muṭahharī dedicates himself to is methodology; he establishes the method first and then goes into the topic. This is a clear characteristic in all of Shahīd Muṭahharī's doctrinal writings, but it comes out most strongly in his discussion of the Imamate. This is due to the topic's importance in the lives of Muslims past and present. We know from political, social, and theological history that the Imamate was the central topic in all of these domains. The Imamate determines the theological and sectarian direction for every Muslim group, and the position from the Imamate necessitates subsequent political and social positions. Thus was the Imamate such that the following saying became a famous one: "No swords in Islam were greater in number than the swords raised about the Imamate."

The question that occurs to many people is this: "Why breathe new life into differences among Muslim groups? What is the need for looking into the Imamate again?" Shahīd Muṭahharī addressed this question at the beginning of this book when he said that when the scholarly methodology is a basis for the discussion, nothing threatens Muslims even if the topic was as dangerous as the Imamate.

A better answer may lie in the following two points:

The discussion of the Imamate is not a discussion of a past historical topic. The Imamate is a principle of faith, or at least it is a headline of an intellectual topic that was of a historical nature at one point. There is a constant need for doctrinal research at all times. For this reason, we should not fall prey to the illusion that the Imamate is a historical topic that does not concern us anymore. True, some concerns of the Imamate, like rulership, are a matter of history. However, the principle and branches of the Imamate are a doctrinal and not a historical issue. Clarifying this point largely depends on the methodology of discussing the Imamate.

The discussion of the Imamate depends on the researcher's methodology. If he chose to consider the Imamate a historical topic, he would deal with it like any past issue. This methodology would definitely force him to raise historical and theological disagreements and look into the endless merits and mistakes of certain individuals.

However, if the researcher chose a methodology that raises the Imamate to its proper level that surpasses the issue of rulership, this would not rekindle past theological and political differences. It would not offend anyone, but rather it would become a bounty that includes all Muslims. This second methodology raises the Imamate to the level of the narration of Imām al-Riḍā ؑ: "The Imamate is the position of the prophets and the inheritance of the trustees. The Imamate is the preserver of religion, the order of the Muslims, the righteousness of this world, and the might of the faithful. The Imamate is Islam's growing root and its elevated branch. Through the Imām, prayer, the *zakāt*, fasting, the pilgrimage, and *jihād* find their completion, and communal spoils (*fayʾ*) and charity become available. Through the Imām, punishments are established, and the frontiers and peripheries are defended." Imām al-Riḍā ؑ adds, "The Imām is like the rising sun that shines its light upon the world." I don't think that any Muslim would oppose the Imamate when it is a sun that shines not only on Muslims but on humanity as a whole.

When the Imamate is raised above sectarian and historical disagreements and theological debates, the Imām ؑ becomes a sun that shines on people and all of creation, and the Imamate regains its position that Imām ʿAlī ؑ described as follows: "I swear by Allah that indeed the earth will never be empty of someone who upholds Allah's proof. He is either visible and well-known or afraid and hidden so that the proofs and evidence of Allah do not be invalidated."

These two points show the purpose of discussing the Imamate. I believe that Shahīd Muṭahharī carefully adhered to both points: he elevated the Imamate from being a historical topic and elevated the Imām from being simply a ruler.

Connection and Not Separation

I spoke a moment ago about the theological method in a way that may imply I was minimizing its importance. The truth is that it's not always the case. The theological methodology is the fruit of great intellectual efforts made by Muslims of all affiliations. Theology, in its pure state, goes back to the time of the Prophet ﷺ: some of his ﷺ *ḥadīths* and arguments have a prominent theological aspect. Islamic theology then underwent a huge shift at the hands of Imām ʿAlī (a) and the Imāms (a) after him, especially Imāms Jaʿfar al-Ṣādiq and ʿAlī al-Riḍā (a). The texts that we have from these two Imāms (a) are highly theological, and that's particularly true in the case of the Imamate. Despite this, Islamic theology, like any other Islamic branch of knowledge, is not uniform. It's full of trends and opinions, which require us to deal with its contents selectively and not accept them wholesale. These observations do not exclude Shīʿī theology and Shīʿī theologians, particularly regarding the Imamate. We should adhere by useful selection and highlight the beneficial writings of the ancients.

This is completely opposite to the silly call of some people to boycott all the works of the ancients and establish entirely new methodologies and branches of knowledge. Establishing methodologies and knowledge cannot begin from square one without relying on previous experience. This cumulative trend is all the more true regarding religious sciences and the foundations of any renaissance. The purpose of these words is not that contemporaries should place their intellects in the hands of the ancients. Absolute acceptance is wrong, and it is equally wrong to boycott the ancients' scholarly and methodological heritage. The correct position is to continue the useful and beneficial heritage of the ancients and highlight it. In the domain of the Imamate in particular, there are innovative attempts and geniuses in contemporary doctrinal research. These attempts include a fair amount of developing and renewing the ideas, ways, and writings of the ancients. When I say "developing," I mean that the seeds of some ideas are taken from the ancients, and when I say "renewing," I mean contemporary researchers' efforts of adding new ideas or completing ideas that lack some components. This is in addition to methodological creativity and the inclusion of the age's questions and concerns into the topic of study.

Some past scholars have engaged in research with extraordinary activity, and we should not simply discount the fruits of their labor by following rash claims. At the level of foundational and argumentative texts, no one can discount the great efforts of Imām ʿAlī 🕮 and the rest of the Imāms 🕮, which are attested in in "Kitāb al-Ḥujja" in *al-Kāfī*. At the level of concepts, proofs, and theoretical frameworks, the modern scholar cannot turn his back on certain rich and innovative efforts or neglect to know about them. These include al-Murtaḍā's *al-Shāfī*, and Shaykh al-Mufīd's *Awāʾil al-maqālāt*, *al-Nukat al-iʿtiqādiyya*, *al-Ifṣāḥ*, and *al-Irshād*. For example, despite *al-Nukat al-iʿtiqādiyya's* brevity, it became a cognitive leaven for subsequent richer writings such as *al-Tajrīd* by Naṣīr al-Dīn al-Ṭūsī, his student and commentator ʿAllāma al-Ḥillī, and those who came after them. Those who call us to boycott these works want us to be like turf that spreads on the surface without having any roots.

The Three Ranks

In his book about the Imamate, Shahīd Muṭahharī begins with the idea that the word Imām itself is not sacred. The Imām is the leader and the head of the people, regardless of whether he is right or wrong. Allah ﷻ says, "We made them Imāms, guiding by Our command,"[1] and "We made them leaders who invite to the Fire."[2] In religious terminology, the ancients define the Imamate as general leadership in the matters of this world and religion. After these quick introductions, Shahīd Muṭahharī speaks about three ranks of Imamate that depend on the role given to the Imām. These three ranks are drawn from the Prophet's ﷺ roles in the *ummah*. His first role was being a prophet connected to heaven, Allah ﷻ, the realm of the unseen, and revelation. In this regard, he was an explainer of the things he received from heaven. In addition, the Prophet ﷺ had another role, which was adjudicating between the Muslims. The Prophet ﷺ usually adjudicated based on apparent proofs in all but exceptional cases, judging according to objective standards. The Prophet ﷺ had another role related to being the ruler of the Muslims, the leader of Islamic society, the guardian of the affairs of the Muslims, and the head of the state. In this regard, the Prophet ﷺ practiced his duties based on Allah's ﷻ permission.

Shahīd Muṭahharī emphasizes the point that in the presence of the Prophet ﷺ, there is no room to ask about the identity of the head of state and the political and social leader of the *ummah*. When the infallible who is guided by heaven is present, no one can precede him in ruling. Based on this clarification, Shahīd Muṭahharī establishes three ranks of the Imamate that depend on the Imām's roles. The first rank includes political and social leadership of the *ummah* and the state, and the guardianship of all Muslims. During his caliphate, Imām ʿAlī ؑ was able to do this. This is the first and lowest rank of the Imamate. Shahīd Muṭahharī is frank and certain enough about his beliefs that he says, "If the Imamate was limited to these boundaries, not exceeding the domain of political leadership

---

[1] Sūrat al-Anbiyāʾ, verse 73.

[2] Sūrat al-Qaṣas, verse 41.

after the Prophet ﷺ, it would've been fairer of us Shīʿa to count it among the branches of faith." However, we do believe in another rank of the Imamate that comes from another role of the Imām. The Imām is the religious authority that explains religion after the Prophet ﷺ.

The idea of religious authority comes from the fact that the noble Prophet ﷺ did not have the chance to explain the entirety of Islam to the entirety of the *ummah* and that the *ummah* needed to fill in the legislative gaps that it started to face after the death of the Prophet ﷺ. At that time, new issues came up due to the expansion of the Islamic world, the Muslims' mixing with other nations, and the development of the civil rule of the state and society. These factors made the *ummah* need a period of time when it would rely on a scholarly authority that meets its needs at the level of religious clarification and legislation. This authority had to be one that received Islam in its complete form from the Prophet ﷺ. This role was given to the Imam after the Prophet ﷺ. It is a role that is more important and critical than the previous role. During his lifetime, the Prophet ﷺ took it upon himself to bring up Imām ʿAlī ؑ and prepare him to fulfill this role.

During the critical period after the death of the Prophet ﷺ, the *ummah* itself needed to refer in religious matters to a perfect, unerring authority. The reason for this is to protect the religion of Allah ﷻ from deviations, analogical reasoning, *ijtihād*, and juristic discretion (*istiḥsān*). The thing that objectively confirms Imām ʿAlī's ؑ competence in performing this role is that everyone went back to him after the death of the Prophet ﷺ. All the caliphs relied on his judgment. This is the rank of the Imamate that requires infallibility, not the first rank. Since infallibility is not something that can be seen, it requires textual proof of the identity of the infallible Imām as the perfect religious authority that reports from the Holy Prophet ﷺ. There are also texts that point to the Imām's ؑ duty as a political ruler and a caliph over the *ummah*. At this point, Shahīd Muṭahharī gets to a critical point in his methodology about the Imamate. He says that if the *ummah* was allowed to choose between a fallible and an infallible Imām, it would be compelled by reason and the Sharia to prefer the infallible Imām. This makes the Imām a religious authority, a political ruler, and a social leader all at once. The important thing about this proposition is that infallibility is not a condition of being the ruler, or else it would've been a constant condition. The ruler should only be infallible if he was an Imām. In other words, every infallible is a ruler but not every ruler is infallible. There has been continual misunderstanding about this issue among Muslims generally, including the Shīʿa. It is thought that the Shīʿa believe in the infallibility of the ruler. However, the truth is that the Shīʿa believe in the infallibility of the Imām who has many duties, one of which is ruling.

If the *ummah* had the choice between an infallible ruler (the Imām) and a fallible ruler, it is not logically and religiously allowed to abandon the infallible ruler for the fallible one. It has already done so in its early history and suffered countless problems as a result. In the case of the twelve Imāms ؑ, the Prophet ﷺ decreed that they are entitled to both roles: political succession (leadership in this world) and religious authority (religious leadership).[3] There is a

---

[3] I would like to benefit from this opportunity to mention some words of Shahīd Muḥammad Bāqir al-Ṣadr that heavily indicate both of these positions and show ʿAlī's ؑ right as appointed by the Prophet ﷺ himself. Shahīd al-Ṣadr says, "… Because the Prophet did not appoint ʿAlī as the highest Muslim authority after him at the social level alone, but also at the intellectual level. There are two-divinely given authorities to Imām ʿAlī. The first is the social authority over the *ummah*, which makes the Imām the actual leader of the Muslims in the social aspects of their lives. The second is the intellectual and legislative authority over the *ummah*, which makes the Imām the highest power after the Book of Allah and the Prophetic precept concerning Islam's rulings, legislations, values, and concepts. The most wonderful Prophetic expression of the first kind of authority was ḥadīth al-Ghadīr and the most wonderful Prophetic expression of the second kind of authority was ḥadīth al-Thaqalayn.

third rank of the Imamate that the two previous ranks do not equal. This rank is the foundation of the Imamate in Shīʿī belief: the Imām has the duty of guardianship, with its moral significance.

In brief, the philosophy of this rank is that a Proof of Allah has to be present on earth at all times. The dimensions of time and space can never be without an Imām. At this point, Shīʿism meets Sufism and mysticism. This is because the Shīʿa believe in the Proof: "Without the Proof, the earth would have swallowed up its inhabitants," the Sufis believe in the Pole, and the mystics believe in the Perfect Man. Based on this methodology, Shahīd Muṭahharī reaches a decisive conclusion, saying, "the Imamate has three ranks. If we do not separate these three ranks, we would have some trouble when we try to make inferences about this topic." As a result, Shahīd Muṭahharī also separates Shīʿism into three ranks. Some Shīʿa believe in the first form of the Imamate (the political Imamate) and others believe in the first and second forms while disbelieving or disregarding the third. Nevertheless, the vast majority of Shīʿī scholars and their adherents believe in the third form as well.[4] However, as Shahīd Muṭahharī says, this is a claim that requires proof. How can we prove its validity? At this point, I leave the reader with the pages of the present book, with all the proofs that it contains.

Main Characteristics

In undertaking this translation, I relied on the seventeenth edition of the book. There may have been other, more recent copies since then. This big number of copies points to something that is greater than the importance, richness, and necessity of the topic itself. I'm

[4] This is according to Shahīd Muṭahharī. However, it seems that the term Twelver (*ithnā ʿashariyya*) refers to groups that accepted the concept of guardianship but differed about its limits, explanation, and meaning.

talking about the author's style. I would describe the book as a study in methodology, and particularly the methodology of approaching the Imamate. The usual methodology in most theological discussions is based on reactions and the examination of the beliefs of the other side. This made the domain of theology full of back-and-forth instead of revolving around foundations. For example, if the other side says the Imamate is determined by election, we respond by saying that it's determined by designation. If the other side denies infallibility and says it's not a condition of the Imām, we hurry to say that it is indeed a condition without differentiating between the ranks of the Imamate in the process. Instead, we ought to establish the foundations of our own creed away from reactions and the sayings of others. After that, we become able to address and respond to allegations.

This foundational characteristic can be found in all the chapters of the book. While setting his foundations, the author does not shy away from explicitly declaring that the doctrine of the Shīʿa about the Imamate is different from the doctrine of the Sunnis. There is another characteristic of Shahīd Muṭahharī's methodology that emerges. Some people have studied the Imamate using the tools of theology while others relied on textual evidence. Others preferred the rational approach. Some contemporaries applied a sociological methodology to the study of the Imamate, while others approached it comparatively. Some researchers even combined more than one methodology. The merit of Shahīd Muṭahharī's methodology is that includes all of these methodologies except the sociological one while keeping its foundational nature and critical spirit.

If I wanted to summarize the most important characteristics of the book, I would say that they are:

Choosing a foundational methodology and explicitly basing the research on our doctrine about the Imamate without any hesitation. The conclusion was that the Imamate is the pillar of Islam and that it is second only to prophethood. The most important component of this point is Shahīd Muṭahharī's three ranks of the Imamate. The degree of a person's Shīʿī belief depends on their belief in these ranks; Shīʿism too has ranks.

Combining the theological, textual, rational, and comparative methodologies into one while distinguishing between the first and third methodology. While the theological methodology relies upon rational tools and proofs, it always moves toward a predetermined outcome. Theology synthesizes the proof for a particular concept. In contrast, the rational methodology follows the dictates of the proof itself and accepts its result. Shahīd Muṭahharī dedicated a chapter for each methodology without neglecting the sayings of the philosophers and the mystics.

Combining clarity and ease with frankness. In the introduction, for example, we notice the author's breadth: he is for unity and against zealousness and closed-mindedness. He agrees to discussing the Imamate as long as the discussion is based on evidence and proofs rather than clinging to empty slogans and going around the same points. It's as though Shahīd Muṭahharī was referring to the problems of the Shīʿī scene that we are facing these days.

Translation Methodology

The problem of most of Shahīd Muṭahharī's intellectual heritage is that it consists of lectures that were recorded on tape and then transcribed. This book is no different. It originally consisted of six lectures that Shahīd Muṭahharī gave in the winter of 1970 at the Muslim Physicians' Union. Anyone familiar with this field knows the pain of working on oral lectures and the difficulty of turning them into an intelligible text. This involves difficulties for the translator that may affect the text. Undoubtedly, part of the coherence of the translation goes back to the coherence of the translator's text. A good text strengthens the translation if the translator did his job correctly.

Since the book was originally a series of lectures, its tone is oratory. I sometimes preserved this tone and sometimes obscured it depending on what fits best with the requirements of a written text. The oratory tone is usually obscured by changing certain pronouns or removing them entirely.

This was the main problem I had while translating. However, I better inform the reader of the following points:

Although the preface was written by the author, it was not intended for this book. Shahīd Muṭahharī wrote it for *Khilāfat va-vilāyat.* The publisher made a good choice when deciding to use it as a preface for this book.

The appendix of the book consists of short commentaries found among Shahīd Muṭahharī's papers and in the notes within the margins of the books he was reading. The publisher chose six such samples to include in the book, but I translated only five into Arabic and excluded the sixth for its irrelevance to Arab readers' interests. I thought it would be better to include these notes at the end of the book and not at the beginning of it as the Persian edition did.

The publisher was the one who chose the book's title. The publisher collected the Shaykh's lectures in a book and chose the title *Imāmat va-giyādat* for the Persian edition. I thought it would be better to limit the title to *al-Imāma.* This is because the Imamate itself is the point that this book revolves around. This point is significant and psychologically effective enough that nothing by its side should be allowed to reduce its effect.

The publisher of the Persian edition titled sections using the phrases "session one, session two, etc." I replaced them with chapter one, chapter two, and so on.

Some historical texts are inaccurate and incidents sometimes get mixed up. This is due to the oral nature of the lectures and the lecturer's task of translating from Arabic into Persian. In some cases, the translation was mixed up with the explanation. I went back to the proper sources to rearrange incidents correctly and certify their wording. I sometimes added a footnote to the words of the author, in which I mentioned the incident verbatim from the historical sources.

I mostly added phrases and sometimes words to connect ideas or clarify them. I indicated them by putting them between brackets or dashes.

The repetition was obvious because the book was a series of oral lectures that were two weeks apart. However, I did not remove any repetitive ideas because they help to instill the point in various ways.

An appealing feature of this book is the audience Q & A after every lecture. The reader will easily notice the boldness of the questions, which indicates the characters of the audience members and the nature of the relationship between them and the lecturer.

Shahīd Muṭahharī has a different series of lectures on the Imamate, which are a practical inquiry into the biographies of the pure Imāms عليهم السلام. Perhaps Allah ﷻ will aid me to translate them some other time.

Dedication

From the very first word I translated in this book, I was eager to dedicate the reward of my efforts to the mother of the pure Imāms عليهم السلام and the daughter of al-Muṣṭafā ﷺ, Fāṭima al-Zahrā' عليها السلام. I now extend my hand, pleading, on a day after a night that is better than a thousand months in the sight of Allah ﷻ. I hope my humble efforts are accepted, eager for al-Zahrā''s عليها السلام intercedence. May Allah ﷻ send His blessings upon her and her father and her husband and her sons and upon the secret endowed in her. My last word is praise to Allah ﷻ, the Lord of all worlds.

Jawād ʿAlī Kassār

(Khālid Tawfīq)

23 Ramaḍān, 1417 AH

بسم الله الرحمن الرحيم

Introduction by the Author[5]

In the Name of Allāh, the Most Gracious, the Most Merciful

Getting into the discussion of the Imamate again may generate the criticism of some readers. For this reason, I thought it best to present and comment on these criticisms. The main criticisms in this regard are two. The first is this: each nation always strives to highlight the positive points of its history, making every effort to cover up any negative points or dark moments. Honorable moments in the history of any religion or movement are a sign of that religion or movement's authenticity and truth, and they increase its appeal. As for unfortunate negative moments in history, they cast doubts on the authenticity of that religion or movement, becoming a weak spot that affects creative energies.

[Arabic translator's note]: The author didn't write these words for this book. They were a preface to the book Khilāfat va-vilāyat by Muḥammad Taqī Sharī'atī, the father of Dr. 'Alī Sharī'atī. The book was published by Ḥusaynniya-ī Irshād in Tehran when the late Shahīd Muṭahharī and the late Sharī'atī worked there together. Given the relation of the preface's ideas to this present book, the publisher chose well when he decided to begin the book with it while removing irrelevant ideas and adding a couple of lines to connect things together.

Frequently discussing the caliphate and the Imamate and the unfortunate incidents of the formative period of Islam weaken the faith of the new generation and its passion for Islam, particularly in our age. This is especially true in light of the spiritual crisis that this generation is going through at the religious level. An objector may say that such discussions might've had advantages in the past, such as causing conversions within Islam. Insisting on these discussions today, however, can shake the pillars and weaken their foundations. Others always strive to cover up the disgraceful parts of their history whereas we Muslims repeat them over and over again and sometimes exaggerate them to make them seem bigger than they really were.

Actually, I cannot agree with the point of view mentioned above. Yes, I do believe that if historical criticism were limited to resurrecting negative incidents and discussing them again, this would lead to results like the ones mentioned above. However, we should also be mindful of the fact that historical criticism does not mean highlighting positive incidents and being content with them while covering up negative ones. Such an approach is not historical criticism but historical distortion. Besides, what history has no negative points and unfortunate incidents? The history of any nation, indeed that of humanity as a whole, is a series of positives and negatives. There is no other possibility.

Allah ﷻ did not create any sinless people or nations like he did with the angels. The difference between the histories of nations, peoples, religions, and sects is not that some are all positive while some are all negative. The difference is in the proportion of positives and negatives.

The Noble Qur'ān showed, in a subtle way, that humans are complex beings with positive and negative characteristics. The angels asked in astonishment about the divine wisdom of making man the vicegerent on earth. Allah ﷻ told them that they only saw the dark side of this being, but that He knows this him, his good characteristics, and his beauty in a way the angels do not.[6] If we wanted to think logically, the history of Islam is unparalleled in the many instances of beauty, humanity, and faith that contains. It is a history full of spirit, brimming with beauty and shining examples, and overflowing with humanity. For this reason, the presence of some dark spots does not diminish Islam's splendid beauty, glory, and greatness.

No nation can claim that the good points in its history outnumber the good points of Islam or that its bad points are less than those of Islam. A Jewish man spoke to ʿAlī ؑ and attempted to blame the Muslims for the incidents of the caliphate during the formative period of Islam, saying, "As soon as you buried your Prophet, you disagreed about him." Imām ʿAlī's ؑ response was beautiful: "We only disagreed about what he said and not about him. As for you, as soon as the water of the sea dried off of your feet, you told your prophet, 'make for us a god like the gods that they have.' He said, 'You are indeed an ignorant lot.'"[7] Imām ʿAlī ؑ was telling the man, "You're wrong. We did not disagree about our Prophet but about what he told us." This means that we disagreed but we had the common ground of believing in monotheism and prophethood. Our disagreement had the following form: does the rule of Islam and the Qurʾān state that it is necessary for the Prophet's ﷺ successor to be an appointed and previously designated person or can he be someone that the *ummah* elects and chooses? As for the

6 Allah ﷻ says, "When your Lord said to the angels, 'Indeed I am going to set a viceroy on the earth,' they said, 'Will You set in it someone who will cause corruption in it, and shed blood, while we celebrate Your praise and proclaim Your sanctity?' He said, 'Indeed I know what you do not know.'" Sūrat al-Baqara, verse 30.

7 *Nahj al-Balāgha*, saying 317. [English translator's note]: Sūrat al-Aʿrāf, verse 138.

Jews, they wanted something that directly opposed the basics of their religion and their Prophet's ﷺ teachings while he was still alive.

In addition, if we suppose that disregarding negative points is fine in regular circumstances, this does not apply to an issue that is at the heart of Islam. It is the basis of Islam because it relates to leadership and the fate of Islamic society depends on it. Disregarding such a thing means disregarding the happiness of the Muslims. Besides, if certain rights were disregarded throughout history, isn't turning a blind eye to that simply an act of assisting the unjust using pen and tongue? This is particularly because these rights belong to people who are the most virtuous members of the *ummah.*

The second criticism is this: what is the fate of Islamic unity if we begin to discuss these issues? The calamity that deprived the Muslims of their might and made them subordinate to non-Muslim nations was precisely due to these sectarian differences between one Muslim group and another. When we look at colonialism in both its old and new form, we realize that the best instrument it had was rekindling these old resentments. The tools of colonialism in all Muslim countries have striven to divide the Muslims in the name of religion and under the pretext of caring about Islam. Aren't the things that already struck us enough? Why should we continue on this same path? Doesn't engaging in such discussions assist colonialism in establishing its goals?

In answer, we say that the thing that the Muslims desperately need today is unity and harmony. These old grudges are the main problem in the Islamic world, and the enemy always benefits from them. However, the objectors to these discussions seem to be confused about the meaning of "Islamic unity." The concept of

"Islamic unity" that was discussed in the past century among Muslim scholars and intellectuals does not mean that Islamic sects should give up their principal and secondary beliefs. What happens is that the common denominators are preserved and the particularities are neglected. Such an approach is neither logical nor practical.

How is it possible to ask the adherents of a certain sect to give up a principle of doctrine or worship in the name of Muslim unity? This is like asking them to disregard a part of Islam in the name of Islam! Causing people to believe in or abandon a certain sect-specific principle can be done in other ways, the most important of which is using logic and proofs. A principle cannot be strengthened or demolished by wishes alone or in the name of common interest. As Shīʿa, we take pride in following Ahl al-Bayt ﷺ, and we are not willing to compromise the smallest thing related to them, including rulings on commendable (*mustaḥabb*) and detestable (*makrūh*) things. We cannot agree with anyone asking us to make compromises, and we do not expect other Muslims to give up any of their principles in the name of common interest and Islamic unity.

What we expect to serve Islamic unity is the creation of an environment of common understanding in which we can present our principles and branches of faith, including our jurisprudence, *ḥadīths,* theology, philosophy, exegesis, and literature. Such an atmosphere allows us to present our ideas as the best ones available. This takes the Shīʿa out of their isolation and opens up important locations in the Muslim world for them. The doors will no longer be locked before the valuable branches of Islamic Shīʿī knowledge. Taking the common elements between all Muslim sects and disregarding their particularities is a violation of the principle of complex consensus (*al-ijmāʿ al-murakkab*).[8] The result of this would definitely be something other than actual Islam. This is because the particularities of any sect are a part of the sum that is Islam. Islam cannot exist in an abstract state form from these characteristics, features, and particularities.

Besides, the pioneers of the lofty idea of Islamic unity themselves do not follow this logic. An example of this among the Shīʿa is Ayatollah Borujerdi ﷺ. Among the Sunnis, there are ʿAllāma Shaykh ʿAbd al-Majīd Salīm and ʿAllāma Shaykh Maḥmūd Shaltūt. These great figures, who are pioneers of Islamic unity, consider that Islamic sects differ in theology, jurisprudence, and other fields while being able to extend the hand of brotherhood to other Muslims and unite against the fierce enemies of Islam. This is due to these sects' commonalities that exceed any differences. This is their version of Islamic unity. These great figures would never call for uniting the sects into one under the pretext of Islamic unity. Such a proposition is not practical at all. In customary terminology, there is a difference between a unified party and a unified front. A unified party requires uniformity among all party members at the level of thought, ideology, methodology, style, and other intellectual particularities. The only exclusion is personal matters. A unified front, however, is when different parties and groups come together as one front based on their commonalities in order to face a common enemy. This takes place despite differences in ideology, path, and method.

---

[8] [English translator's note]: The principle of complex consensus happens when jurists agree on a ruling while differing about its reasons. This means that the ruling changes based on the reasons that the jurists accept or reject, which effectively nullifies the consensus. For example, there is a consensus among the Ḥanafis and the Shāfiʿīs on the ruling that vomit and coming in contact with it violate the state of ritual purity (*ṭahāra*). However, the violating factor for the Ḥanafis is the vomit itself, whereas the violating factor for the Shāfiʿīs is the touching of it. If touching the vomit did not violate ritual purity for al-Shāfiʿī, there would no longer be consensus about the issue and vice versa. See al-Jurjānī, *Muʿjam al-taʿrīfāt*, definition 33: "*al-ijmāʿ al-murakkab*," 12.

Obviously, there is no contradiction between forming a unified rank against the enemy and insisting on defending one's individual school while critiquing other brothers' schools and calling those who are in one front to one's own school. What Ayatollah Borujerdi ﷶ particularly had in mind was establishing the proper atmosphere to spread the knowledge of Ahl al-Bayt ﷺ among our Sunni brothers. He believed that this cannot be done except by setting up a common ground. The success of the late Borujerdi ﷶ in having some books of Shīʿī jurisprudence printed in Egypt by the Egyptians themselves was the result of this understanding. This was the greatest success of the Shīʿa's scholars. In any case, supporting the cause of Islamic unity does not require falling short in declaring the truth. We should guard against exciting the emotions, biases, and ill feelings of the other side. As for scholarly discussions, they deal with reason and logic and have nothing to do with feelings and emotions. Luckily, our present age witnessed the presence of many skilled Shīʿī scholars who follow this methodology. The most important of them are the eminent ʿAllāma Ayatollah Sayyid ʿAbd al-Ḥusayn Sharaf al-Dīn al-ʿĀmilī ﷶ, the great ʿAllāma Shaykh Muḥammad Ḥusayn Kāshif al-Ghiṭā' ﷶ, and the eminent ʿAllāma Ayatollah Shaykh ʿAbd al-Ḥusayn al-Amīnī ﷶ, who is the author of *al-Ghadīr.*

The severely neglected biography of Imām ʿAlī ﷺ is the best lesson in unity at the levels of his sayings and actions. Imām ʿAlī ﷺ did not hold back from demanding his rights and speaking out against those who deprived him ﷺ of them. Imām ʿAlī ﷺ was very honest about this, and his desire for Islamic unity was never an obstacle. Many sermons in *Nahj al-Balāgha* attest to this. At the same time, these grievances did not cause the Imām ﷺ to divide the Muslim front that was united against external enemies. Imām ʿAlī ﷺ participated in communal and Friday prayers and took his portion of the spoils.

He spared no effort to guide the caliphs, and he always advised them when consulted.

During the Muslim-Sassanid wars, the caliph at the time [ʿUmar b. al-Khaṭṭāb] wanted to go to battle himself. When he consulted Imām ʿAlī ﷺ about this, the Imām ﷺ told him not to. The reason, Imām ʿAlī ﷺ said, was that if the Muslim army were defeated, the enemy would believe that reinforcements were coming from Medina. However, if the caliph personally went out to fight, the enemy would say, "'This is the head of the Arabs. Cut him off and things would be easy for you.' This would be a worse alternative due to their eagerness to have you dead."[9] This was Imām ʿAlī's ﷺ method in practice as well. On the one hand, he did not agree to assume any responsibility assigned to him at the level of the military, the provinces, the pilgrimage, or other levels. Accepting these positions would have meant that he has given up his established right. In other words, if he ﷺ had accepted any post, this would have exceeded simply preserving the spirit of harmony, general cooperation, and Islamic unity. While the Imām ﷺ personally refused to accept any positions, he did not forbid his followers and relatives from accepting them because their acceptance is not equivalent to validating the caliphate. It only signifies cooperation and harmony.[10]

---

[9] [Arabic translator's note]: *Nahj al-Balāgha*, sermon 144. I replaced the author's explanation with the verbatim Arabic text. Imām ʿAlī ﷺ told ʿUmar, "The head of the Islamic order is as a thread is to the beads, gathering them and keeping them together. If the thread was broken, the beads would scatter everywhere and some of them would be lost for good ... Be like the axis that moves the Arabs and makes them go into the furnace of war on your behalf ... If the non-Arabs saw you, they would say, 'This is the head of the Arabs. Cut him off and things would be easy for you.' This would be a worse alternative due to their eagerness to have you dead."

[10] See the Imām's ﷺ letter number 62 in Ibn Abī al-Ḥadīd, *Sharḥ Nahj al-Balāgha*: "I held back until I saw people turning their backs on Islam."

Imām ʿAlī 🕮 was very particular in this regard. This is a sign of his dedication to the goals of Islam. He always fixed and righted other people's wrongs. Abū Sufyān wanted to take advantage of the Imām's 🕮 refusal and avenge himself from the Prophet 🕮 through his trustee 🕮. However, ʿAlī's 🕮 heart was too sharp-sighted to be deceived by Sufyānī tricks, so he 🕮 refused Abū Sufyān's offer and threw him out.[11] The likes of Abū Sufyān and Ḥayy b. Akhṭab exist in every time and place. Ḥayy b. Akhṭab is showing himself again during our time in many different trends. The Muslims, and particularly the Shīʿa and people who accept Imām ʿAlī's 🕮 guardianship, should make the Imām's 🕮 life and precept their example and not be deceived by Abū Sufyān and Ḥayy b. Akhṭab.[12]

These were the objections that are raised against such discussions, and this was our response and point of view. However, it's astonishing that there are some people who object for the sake of objecting. This group hopes that the Imamate and the caliphate would be a constant topic of talk and discussion without actually generating anything new. This is done by turning the caliphate and the Imamate into slogans and redundancies, steering away from useful analytical methods that are supported with evidence. The former method makes emotions run high, but it does not satisfy or strengthen the mind. This is precisely what the enemy wants. If the discussion was presented in an analytical manner, there would be

---

11 [Arabic translator's note]: This was when Abū Sufyān offered to support Imām ʿAlī 🕮 by filling the battlefield with horses and men against the then-present caliphate.

12 Imām ʿAlī 🕮 himself mentioned several times that he put up with a lot to safeguard the unity of the Muslims and prevent their division. An example of this is his saying, "There are things that happened, and we chose patience although we were greatly wronged, out of submission to Allah's command through which He tested us. We did this in hope of gaining its reward. Having patience was better than the division of the Muslims and the shedding of their blood." In another sermon, he says, "By Allah, if I didn't worry about the division of the Muslims and the return of most of them to faithlessness, which would affect the religion, I would have changed the situation to the best of my ability." See al-Irshād, 1/246, 249.

no justification for turning it into a topic of constant back-and-forth.

The Meanings and Ranks of the Imamate

Our discussion revolves around the Imamate (*al-imāma*). We know that the issue of the Imamate has great importance among us Shīʿa, which is not paralleled among other Muslims. The secret to this distinction goes back to the difference in the concept of the Imamate between the Shīʿa and other groups of Muslims.

There are similarities of course, but the Shīʿa's beliefs about the Imamate have unique components that make it extraordinarily important to them.

For example, when we Shīʿa want to count the principles of faith (*uṣūl al-dīn*) from our own perspective, we say that they are monotheism (al-*tawḥīd*), prophethood (*al-nubuwwa*), justice (*al-ʿadl*), the Imamate, and the Day of Return (*al-maʿād*). The Imamate, for us, is one of the principles of faith.

For their part, Ahl al-Sunnah profess the Imamate in a certain form; they do not categorically deny it. However, the form of Imamate that they believe in does not elevate the concept to the rank of a principle of faith; they view it only as one of the branches (*farʿ*, pl. *furūʿ*).

This means that there is a disagreement about the Imamate. The Sunnis believe in one form of the Imamate and we believe in another form. The question that poses itself here is: "Why did the Shīʿa elevate the Imamate to the position of a principle of faith while the Sunnis considered it one of the branches?"

This goes back to the difference in the conception of the Imamate among the Shīʿa and the Sunnis, which I mentioned earlier.

The Meaning of the Imām

The word Imām does not have a sacred connotation in itself. An Imām is someone who leads; he is imitated and followed. He is the person who heads a group that follows him, regardless of whether he is a just supporter of the straight path or a misguided supporter of falsehood.[13]

The Noble Qurʾān uses the term Imām to refer to both groups. In one place, it says: "We made them Imāms, guiding by Our command,"[14] while in another it says, "We made them leaders who invite to the Fire."[15]

Speaking of Firʿawn, the Qurʾān uses a word equivalent to the word Imām: "On the Day of Resurrection he will lead [*yaqdumu*] his people."[16]

This means that an Imām is a person who is followed. In this discussion, we won't concern ourselves with the misguided Imām but rather with the concept of Imām in general.

The Imamate has several meanings. The Sunnis believe in some of these meanings despite disagreeing with us about the form of the Imamate and the identity of the Imām, but they deny some of its meanings entirely. It's not simply that they believe in all the

---

[13] [Arabic translator's note]: In *al-Mufradāt,* we find: "The Imām is a person who leads and is imitated in words, deeds, or writing, regardless of whether he is right or wrong. Its plural is *aʾimma. Al-Mufradāt,* 20. *Al-Siḥāḥ* contains the following definition: "The Imām is someone who leads; the plural is *aʾimma.*" See *al-Siḥāḥ*, 5/1865. The definition in *Lisān al-ʿarab* is this: "The Imām of a people is the leader and head, such as when you say, 'The Imām of the Muslims.'" *Lisān al-ʿarab*, 12/26.

[14] Sūrat al-Anbiyāʾ, verse 73.

[15] Sūrat al-Qaṣas, verse 41.

[16] Sūrat Hūd, verse 98.

meanings that we believe in while disagreeing with us about the identity of the Imām.

They differ with us about the manner and form of the Imamate and the identity of the Imām. The Imamate that they believe in has the meaning of presiding over a group. The books of the theologians of old (*al-mutakallimūn,* sing. *mutakallim*) contain such a meaning or ones close to it.

In his *al-Tajrīd,* Naṣīr al-Dīn al-Ṭūsī defines the Imamate as being "a general leadership (*riyāsa ʿāmma*)."

At this point of the discussion, it seems crucial to speak of a certain matter.

The Noble Prophet's Concerns

Given the noble Prophet's ﷺ unique position in Islam, he had multiple concerns and responsibilities relating to his own time according to the Qurʾān and his biography. He had many responsibilities and duties simultaneously.

The Prophet's ﷺ first responsibility was being a prophet of Allah ﷻ; he assumed this responsibility and performed it on the ground. The meaning of this is that he ﷺ explained the divine rulings and the heavenly teachings. The Qurʾān says, "Take whatever the Prophet gives you, and relinquish whatever he forbids you."[17] The verse means that the rulings and teachings explained by the Prophet ﷺ came from Allah ﷻ. In this position, the only thing a prophet can do is explain the revelation.

---

[17] Sūrat al-Ḥashr, verse 7.

Another position that the Prophet ﷺ assumed was the position of judge. He was a judge among the Muslims.

From the Islamic perspective, judging is not an arbitrary duty that anyone can perform, judging between contenders. Judging in Islam is a heavenly affair because it requires ruling according to the dictates of justice. A judge is the one who issues rulings and settles disagreements and differences fairly.

This position was assigned to the Prophet ﷺ according to the Qurʾān: "But no, by your Lord! They will not believe until they make you a judge in their disputes, then do not find within their hearts any dissent to your verdict and submit in full submission." [18]This means that Allah ﷻ gave the Prophet ﷺ the right to settle people's differences and judge between them.

This position that the Prophet ﷺ had was a divine position and not an earthly one; the Prophet ﷺ was truly a judge who adjudicated between people on the ground.

The third position that the Prophet ﷺ had, which was also assigned to him by the Qurʾān and which he actually practiced, was the position of general leadership.

The Prophet ﷺ was the leader and the head of the Muslim community. In other words, he was their ruler (*sāʾis*). Some scholars have mentioned that Allah ﷻ alluded to this responsibility in the verse: "O you who have faith! Obey Allah and obey the Prophet and those vested with authority among you."[19] This verse proves, [O

---

[18] Sūrat al-Nisāʾ, verse 65.

[19] Sūrat al-Nisāʾ, verse 59.

Muslims], that the Prophet ﷺ is your leader and the head of your community.

When we speak of the three concerns of the Prophet ﷺ, we are not speaking metaphorically and attributing positions to the Prophet ﷺ without a basis.

At the level of the first concern, the Prophet's ﷺ words are only a result of divine revelation. Here, the Prophet ﷺ has no choice in the matter; his only duty is to make Allah's ﷻ commands known, and he is only a means of communication. An example of this are the commands that the Prophet ﷺ revealed regarding the teachings of Islam such as performing the prayers and fasting, among other rulings.

The judgments he made among people, however, did not take the form of a revelation. When a disagreement arose between two people, the Prophet ﷺ judged between them according to the standards of Islam, and he chose one of them as the rightful party. In this case, Jibrāʾīl did not descend with a revelation to clear up the issue. Revelation did interfere in special cases, however.

The general rule in this regard is that the Prophet's ﷺ judgment takes place based on apparent evidence, just like anyone else's judgment. The only difference is that the Prophet's ﷺ judgment is the best judgment of all.

The Prophet ﷺ himself mentioned that he judges based on apparent evidence. This means that a case brought before him had a plaintiff and a defendant. The plaintiff had to bring forth two just witnesses (*shāhidān ʿadlān*, sing. *shāhid ʿadl*) to testify to the truth of his claims. After that, the Prophet ﷺ made his ruling based upon apparent evidence; this ruling reflected the Prophet's ﷺ judgment and not a divine revelation.

Regarding the third concern, the Prophet ﷺ did his duties from his position as a leader of society. If he commanded something from this position, this prophetic command would be separate from the revelation of Allah ﷻ. Allah ﷻ gave the Prophet ﷺ this right and this leadership role.

The Prophet ﷺ practiced the prerogatives (*ṣalāḥiyyāt,* sing. *ṣalāḥiyya*) of his position as a leader. For this reason, he ﷺ sometimes consulted his companions. In battles such as Badr, Uḥud, and many others, the noble Prophet ﷺ consulted his companions. In contrast, the rulings of Allah ﷻ do not allow for consultation. Did you ever hear that the Prophet ﷺ consulted his companions about the sunset (*maghrib*) prayer? When his ﷺ companions spoke to him about promulgating the commands of Allah ﷻ, he always said that the matter was not up to him but to Allah ﷻ. This was the only way that things could be.

In issues relating to leading and managing society, the Prophet ﷺ sometimes consulted his companions and asked for their opinions.

We can conclude from what has been said that if the noble Prophet ﷺ commanded something in the domain of leadership, it was one of the prerogatives given to him by Allah ﷻ. If revelation ever interfered in a special administrative or executive case that was among the prerogatives of leadership, this interference was an exception and not a general rule. All the Prophet's ﷺ executive and managerial duties as head and leader of society were commanded through revelation. At this rank too, the Prophet ﷺ was only a deliverer of revelation.

The above definitively proves that the noble Prophet ﷺ had all these concerns, positions, and titles at the same time.

The Imamate as Leadership of Society

In the first meaning that I mentioned, the Imamate is general leadership. This means that one of the positions that were left empty after the Prophet's ﷺ passing is the position of leader. Society needs a leader; that is an undoubtable fact. The question that arises is this: "Who is the leader of society after the Prophet ﷺ?

Both the Shīʿa and the Sunnis agree on this principle; just as a Shīʿī believes in the necessity of senior leadership in society, so does a Sunni.

This was the reason behind the historical and theological significance of the issue of the caliphate. The Shīʿa believe that the Prophet ﷺ himself appointed his successor and declared that the affairs of the Muslims should be under the command of ʿAlī ؑ, whereas the Sunnis followed a different logic that led them not to accept this proposition. At least, they did not accept the Shīʿī view of the caliphate, saying that the Prophet ﷺ did not appoint a specific successor, but rather that the Muslims themselves had the duty of electing the leader who was to succeed the Prophet ﷺ.

This means that the Sunnis also accept the principle of the Imamate when it has the meaning of leadership, believing in the necessity of an Imām according to the method mentioned earlier. The Shīʿa disagree with the Sunnis about this, believing in the Imamate by appointment (*taʿyīn*). The Shīʿa believe that the noble Prophet ﷺ himself appointed the Imām after him through divine revelation.

If the Imamate was limited to these boundaries, not exceeding the domain of political leadership after the Prophet ﷺ, it would've been fairer of us Shīʿa to count it among the branches of faith. In that case, we could've said the Imamate is a secondary issue (*masʾala farʿiyya*) like the prayer for instance. However, the Imamate that the Shīʿa believe in is not limited to these boundaries. They don't only believe that Imām ʿAlī ؑ is one of the Prophet's ﷺ companions, that he is better and more knowledgeable, pious, and worthy than Abū Bakr, ʿUmar, ʿUthmān, and hundreds of other companions, including Salmān and Abū Dharr, and that the Prophet ﷺ himself appointed him ؑ to assume the caliphate.

No, the Shīʿa don't stop at this; they believe in two other issues that the Sunnis don't believe in and don't attribute to Imām ʿAlī ؑ. One of these issues is the Imamate that has the meaning of religious authority (*al-marjaʿiyya al-dīniyya*).

The Imamate as Religious Authority

We mentioned that the Prophet ﷺ was a deliverer of revelation. The people referred to him in their questions about the details of Islam that weren't mentioned in the Qurʾān. The question here is whether the contents of the Qurʾān and the teachings of the Prophet ﷺ are the sum of Islamic rulings, commands, and knowledge. Did the limitations of time mean that the things that the Prophet ﷺ taught the people did not constitute the totality of Islamic rulings?

Imām ʿAlī ؑ was the Prophet's ﷺ trustee (*waṣī*, pl. *awṣiyā*), and the Prophet ﷺ taught him everything about Islam, instructed him about what is and what should be, and told him about the generalities (*kulliyyāt*) of Islam. The Prophet ﷺ nurtured Imām ʿAlī ؑ in these teachings, so Imām ʿAlī ؑ turned into an exceptional scholar who exceeded all his contemporaries. He became like the Prophet ﷺ: he was never incorrect or confused, and he knew about all things that had to do with Allah ﷻ.

The Prophet ﷺ brought Imām ʿAlī ؑ before the *ummah* and commanded the people to refer to this trustee and the trustees after him in the matters of their religion.

In this regard, the Imamate is actually a kind of specialization and insight about Islam. However, it's a much more elaborate specialization than that of the *mujtahid*. It's a specialization that comes from Allah ﷻ. This means that the Imāms ؑ are specialists in Islam. However, their specialization was not a result of their own intellects and thought because such knowledge is necessarily subject to error. The Imāms ؑ received the knowledge of Islam from the Prophet ﷺ by a method of the unseen (*al-ghayb*) that we are not familiar with.

The knowledge of the Prophet ﷺ went to Imām ʿAlī ؑ and then to the Imāms ؑ after him. Throughout all the Imāms' ؑ lives, there has always been an infallible (*maʿṣūm*) kind of Islamic knowledge that gets transferred to the succeeding Imām.

The Sunnis do not accord this status to any person; they do not believe in this rank of the Imamate. It's not that they believe in it but accord it to Abū Bakr and not Imām ʿAlī ؑ.

They do not believe in the status of infallible knowledge in regard to Abū Bakr, ʿUmar, ʿUthmān, or any other companion. This is why their books relate thousands of mistakes in religious matters that were committed by Abū Bakr and ʿUmar. In contrast, the Shīʿa believe in the infallibility (*ʿiṣma*) of their Imāms ؑ; they would never attribute error to any Imām.

Among the things that Ahl al-Sunnah mention in their books is that Abū Bakr once said after he made a mistake, "There is a devil that takes hold of me."[20] As for ʿUmar, he made a mistake once and said, "Even women are more knowledgeable than ʿUmar."[21]

It is also mentioned that when Abū Bakr died, his family members cried and wailed. Among the wailer was ʿĀʾisha, the Prophet's ﷺ wife and Abū Bakr's daughter. When the crying and wailing from Abū Bakr's house reached a peak and ʿUmar heard about it, he sent word ordering the women to stop. He repeated his prohibition and threatened to beat the wailing women with his stick. At that point, ʿĀʾisha sent for him to come to the house himself. When he came to her, she asked him the reason for his behavior, so he said that he

---

[20] [Arabic translator's note]: Abū Bakr's words, according to the historians, are as follows: "There is a devil that takes hold of me. If I am upright, assist me, and if I deviate, set me straight." See *al-Ṣawāʿiq*, 7; *al-Imāma wal-siyāsa*, 1/2; *Sharḥ Nahj al-Balāgha*, 2/8. In *Sharḥ Nahj al-Balāgha*, it's mentioned that Abū Bakr prefaced his saying with the following words, "O people, I became ruler over you although I am not the best of you, so if I do well, assist me, and if I do ill, set me straight. There is a devil that takes hold of me."

[21] [Arabic translator's note]: The author is referring to the well-known incident of ʿUmar's conversation with the woman about the impermissibility of setting expensive dowries (*ṣidāq*). Al-Zamakhsharī mentions this in his *al-Kashshāf*: "ʿUmar stood up to preach and said, 'O people, do not set expensive dowries. If expensive dowries were a merit in this world or an expression of piety, the Prophet ﷺ would've been more entitled than you to such merit and piety. The dowries of the Prophet's ﷺ wives never exceeded twelve ounces.' A woman stood up and said to ʿUmar, 'Why are you denying us a right given to us by Allah ﷻ when He ﷻ said, 'And you have given one of them a quintal [of gold]'? ʿUmar then said, 'Everyone knows more than ʿUmar does.'" See *al-Kashshāf*, 1/514. As for Ibn Abī al-Ḥadīd, he says, "He [meaning ʿUmar] once said, 'If I hear of a woman whose dowry exceeds the dowry offered by the Prophet ﷺ, I will take the excess from her.' A woman said to him, 'Allah does not permit you. Allah ﷻ said, 'And you have given one of them a quintal [of gold], do not take anything away from it. Would you take it by way of calumny and flagrant sin?!' He said, 'Everyone knows more than ʿUmar does, even the wearers of anklets [women]. Isn't it amazing that an Imām made a mistake and a woman was correct? She beat your Imām with her argument.'" *Sharḥ Nahj al-Balāgha*, 2/113. In fact, ʿUmar often made such statements on different occasions. Another example is that he once passed by a young man of the Helpers (*anṣār*). ʿUmar was thirsty and he asked the young man for water, so the latter mixed up a drink of water and honey for him. ʿUmar refused to drink it and said, "Allah says, 'You have exhausted your good things in the life of the world.' The youth responded, 'O Commander of the Believers, this verse is neither about you nor about any of the Muslims. Recite the sentence that precedes it: 'The day when the faithless are exposed to the Fire, [they will be told,] 'You have exhausted your good things in the life of the world.' ʿUmar then said, 'All people are more knowledgeable than ʿUmar.'" See *Sharḥ Nahj al-Balāgha*, 3/96.

heard the Prophet ﷺ say, "A dead person is punished when his relatives cry for him." ʿĀʾisha told ʿUmar that this ḥadīth had a story behind it and that he was mistaken: the story was that a Jew died and his relatives cried for him, so the Prophet ﷺ said that the man was being punished while his relatives cried for him. He did not say that the man was being punished because his relatives were crying for him. This means that the two incidents weren't related.[22]

Besides, if crying for dead people is prohibited (ḥarām), the criers are the ones committing a bad deed; what fault did the dead person commit to be punished for the mistakes of others?

After ʿUmar listened to ʿĀʾisha, he was amazed and said that he would've been doomed if it were not for women's judgment.

Ahl al-Sunnah also mention that ʿUmar said multiple times, "ʿUmar would have been doomed without ʿAlī." This is because Imām ʿAlī ؑ corrected ʿUmar's mistakes, and ʿUmar himself admitted it. This means that the Sunnis don't believe in this rank of the Imamate. The importance of this issue goes back to the idea that the revelation was restricted to the Prophet ﷺ.

We don't say that the Imāms ؑ received divine revelation. The only person to deliver Islam to humanity was the Prophet ﷺ, and

---

22 [Arabic translator's note]: Imām al-Nawawī mentioned in his commentary on Saḥīḥ Muslim that all the narrations on the punishment of the dead due to the tears of the living go back to ʿUmar b. al-Khaṭṭāb and his son ʿAbdullāh. Sayyida ʿĀʾisha denounced this and said that ʿUmar and his son must've misremembered or gotten mixed up. Her proof was the verse: "No bearer shall bear another's burden." Concerning the incident when ʿUmar prevented ʿĀʾisha and Abū Bakr's family from crying for him, al-Ṭabarī mentions that ʿĀʾisha wailed for her father: "When Abū Bakr died, ʿĀʾisha wailed for him. ʿUmar b. al-Khaṭṭāb came to her door and forbade the women from crying for Abū Bakr but they refused. ʿUmar told Hishām b. al-Walīd, 'Go in there and bring me Abū Bakr's sister, the daughter of Ibn Abī Quḥāfa.' When she heard that, ʿĀʾisha told Hishām, 'I forbid you to enter my house.' ʿUmar then told him, 'I gave you permission. Go inside.' Hishām went in and brought out Abū Bakr's sister Umm Farwa to ʿUmar, and the latter hit her multiple times with his stick. When they heard about it, the mourners dispersed." See al-Ṭabarī, 2/614.

Allah ﷻ taught His Prophet ﷺ everything that had to be known in Islam. It's not that some of Islam's teachings weren't revealed to the Prophet ﷺ; it was a question of whether there were any Islamic rulings that the Prophet ﷺ didn't manage to communicate to the people.

The Sunnis believe that the rulings of Islam are limited to the rulings that the Prophet ﷺ communicated to his companions. Confusion spread when issues that were not mentioned in narrations from the companions came up. From this vacuum came analogical reasoning (*qiyās*) to fill the gaps. Imām ʿAlī ؑ says in *Nahj al-Balāgha* about this, "Did Allah reveal a deficient religion such that He required their assistance to complete it?"

In contrast, the Shīʿa believe that Allah ﷻ did not reveal a deficient religion to His ﷻ Prophet ﷺ and that the Prophet ﷺ did not omit anything of the divine revelation in his explanations to the people. However, the totality of the rulings that the Prophet ﷺ delivered did not equal his sayings to the people. In other words, the rulings that reached the people did not express the totality of the rulings that were revealed to the Prophet ﷺ by Allah ﷻ. The formulation of the rulings in their totality was left to the Prophet's ؑ special student, Imām ʿAlī b. Abī Ṭālib ؑ, who was ordered to explain things to the people. In addition, the subject matter of many rulings did not emerge during the time of the Prophet ﷺ; these things came up later.

From this point arises the issue of infallibility. The Shīʿa say that since the Prophet ﷺ cannot intentionally or unintentionally commit mistakes or get confused, his special student should be the same. Just like the Prophet ﷺ is aided by a form of divine direction (*tasdīd ilāhī*), his special student is aided by it too.

This is another rank of the Imamate.

The Imamate as Guardianship

There's a third rank of the Imamate, and it is the pinnacle of the concept of the Imamate. The books of the Shīʿa abound with this understanding of the Imamate, which is a common factor between Shiism and Sufism.

When I say that this rank of the Imamate expresses a common understanding, I don't want to be misunderstood. You might've come across the words of Orientalists who also portray the matter in this light.

The issue that this rank of the Imamate reflects was extensively discussed by the mystics (*ʿurafāʾ*, sing. *ʿārif*), and it was well-known among the Shīʿa since the formative period of Islam. I still remember that Henry Corbin asked ʿAllāma Ṭabāṭabāʾī in a conversation that took place ten years ago whether the Shīʿa appropriated this concept from the Sufis or the other way around. Corbin's point was that one side borrowed the concept from another. ʿAllāma Ṭabāṭabāʾī told him that the Sufis were the ones who borrowed the concept from the Shīʿa because it was widespread among the Shīʿa at a time when Sufism hadn't yet formed. It was only later that the concept made it into the Sufi context and became widespread there.

We can conclude from this that if one of the two sides borrowed the concept from the other, which is an unavoidable inference, the Sufis were the ones who borrowed the concept from the Shīʿa.

The concept I am talking about here is the concept of the Perfect Man (*al-insān al-kāmil*), or the Proof of the Age (*ḥujjat al-ʿaṣr*).

The gnostics and Sufis focused extensively on the idea of the Perfect Man. Rūmī says, "Every age has a guardian (*walī*) of its own." In every era, there is a Perfect Man who carries within him the general morality of humanity (*al-maʿnawiyya al-insāniyya al-ʿāmma*). No time is without the perfect guardian, who is sometimes called the Pole (*al-quṭb*).

The Sufis believe that the perfect guardian has perfect human qualities and stations (*maqāmāt*, sing. *maqām*) that we cannot even comprehend. Of these stations is his authority over consciences (*ḍamāʾir*, sing. *ḍamīr*), or hearts (*qulūb*, sing *qalb*), due to his being a universal soul (*rūh kulliyya*) that encompasses all souls. In this regard, Rūmī mentions the story of Ibrāhīm b. Adham, which is a mythical story. Rūmī often used myths to express his ideas.

Rūmī's goal wasn't to report historical facts; he used myths to express his ideas. In this context, he mentions that Ibrāhīm b. Adham passed by the sea and threw a needle in it. He then sought his needle, and all the fish of the sea peeped their heads out of the water, each with a needle in its mouth.

The issue of guardianship (*wilāya*) is usually mentioned in the Shīʿī context in a similar but much more powerful way. In Shiism, the guardian is the Proof of the Time (*ḥujjat al-zamān*) such that no time is ever without the Proof: "Without the Proof, the earth would have swallowed up its inhabitants." This means that the earth has never been and will never be without the Perfect Man. The Shīʿa believe that this Perfect Man has many stations and ranks (*darajāt*, sing. *daraja*). In most of the visitations (*ziyārāt*, sing. *ziyāra*) that we read, we admit this kind of guardianship and Imamate; we believe that our Imāms عليهم السلام have such universal souls.

In the visitation that we read all the time, which constitutes one of the pillars of Shīʿism, we say, "I bear witness that you witness me standing here, hear my speech, and return my salutations." We speak to our Imām ﷺ like this although he is deceased; there is no difference in this station whether he is alive or dead. This doesn't mean that this is a unique quality of the Imām ﷺ after death and that he ﷺ wasn't also like this in life.

I would say, for example, "Peace be upon you, O ʿAlī b. Mūsā al-Riḍā," then I would bear witness and admit that he hears my speech and returns my salutations.

Ahl al-Sunna, with the exception of the Wahābīs, only attribute this station to the noble Prophet ﷺ; they only believe in spiritual elevation and breadth in this world in regards to the Prophet ﷺ. As for us Shīʿa, this doctrine is one of the principles of our school that we steadfastly adhere to.

It's clear from the above that the Imamate has three ranks. If we do not separate these three ranks, we would have some trouble when we try to make inferences about this topic.

This also means that Shīʿism has three ranks. Some Shīʿa believe in the Imamate only in its meaning of social leadership. This group of Shīʿa believes that the Prophet ﷺ appointed Imām ʿAlī ﷺ as leader after him, and that Abū Bakr, ʿUmar, and ʿUthmān stepped forward of their own accord, contrary to the Prophet's ﷺ wishes. These people are Shīʿa to this extent only; they either don't believe in the two other ranks or are silent about them.

Other groups of Shīʿa believe in the second rank of the Imamate as well, but not in the third. In this regard, it is said that the late Sayyid Muḥammad Bāqir Darchiʾī, Sayyid Borujerdi's ﷺ teacher in Iṣfahān, denied the third rank; he believed in the Imamate in its two ranks but did not go all the way to the third.

The majority of the Shīʿa and their scholars, however, believe in the third rank as well.

If we want to look into the topic of the Imamate, it has to be done in three stages. We have to examine the Imamate according to the Qurʾān, the Imamate according the Prophetic precept (*al-sunnah*), and the Imamate according to reason (*ʿaql*).

In the first stage, we need to see whether the Qurʾānic verses about the Imamate signify the Imamate as the Shīʿa believe in it. If the verses do signify this belief, are they limited to the meanings of political and social leadership or do they also signify the Imamate as religious authority and even moral guardianship?

When we wrap up the discussion of the Imamate according to the Qurʾān, we will move on to the Imamate according the Prophetic precept to see what it says. Afterward, we will analyze it according to the rules of logical reasoning to see reason's view of it and examine whether reason accepts it in all three stages. Will the judgment of reason favor Ahl al-Sunnah at the level of social leadership, stating that the Prophet's ﷺ successor must be elected through communal consultation (*shūrā*), or will it state that the Prophet ﷺ should appoint his successor himself? After that, we will move on to see what reason has to say about the two other ranks.

A Ḥadīth About the Imamate

Before we mention the verses of the Qurʾān that discuss the Imamate, I will relate to you a well-known *ḥadīth* that is narrated both by the Sunnis and the Shīʿa. Usually, when both groups agree on the narration of a *ḥadīth,* this is significant. If both the Sunnis and the Shīʿa agree on the narration of a *ḥadīth* through different channels, this is an almost sure sign that it was definitively (*qaṭʿī*) uttered by the Prophet ﷺ or the Imām ﵇.

There is a variation in the wording of the *ḥadīth* between the two groups, but the meaning is basically the same. As Shīʿa, we often narrate it in the following way: "Whoever dies without knowing the Imām of his time will die a pre-Islamic death (*mīta jāhiliyya*)."[23] The words of the *ḥadīth* have a strong and powerful meaning and significance because prior to Islam people were polytheists and did not believe in monotheism and prophethood.

This *ḥadīth* frequently appears in the books of the Shīʿa, and it conforms to their principles of faith entirely. The *ḥadīth* appears in *al-Kāfī,* which is the most important *ḥadīth* book that the Shīʿa have.

The important thing here is that the *ḥadīth* appears in the books of Ahl al-Sunna; their books on *ḥadīth* narrated it in the following way: "Whoever dies without an Imām will die a pre-Islamic death."[24] It also occurred in the following way: "Whoever dies without pledging allegiance to anyone will die a pre-Islamic death."[25] Ahl al-Sunnah also frequently used the Shīʿa wording as well as the following formulation: "Whoever dies without having an Imām will die a pre-Islamic death."

The *ḥadīth* is strongly-worded to signify the great importance that the noble Prophet ﷺ gave to the issue of the Imamate.

---

[23] *Dalāʾil* al-Ṣadūq, 6, 13.

[24] *Musnad Aḥmad.*

[25] [Arabic translator's note]: *Ṣaḥīḥ Muslim,* 3/1478

Those who only believe in the Imamate as social leadership base themselves on the Noble Prophet's ﷺ emphasis on the aspect of social leadership. The Prophet ﷺ raised the issue of social leadership to such a level that any *ummah* that does not have a leader and Imām is an *ummah* that dies on the path of pre-Islam. This is because the correct explanation and implementation of the rulings of Islam is closely related to rightful leadership and the community's connection to its leader.

Islam is not an individualistic religion that allows a person to say, "I believe in Allah and the Prophet , but I don't care about everyone else." No. In addition to your belief in Allah ﷻ and the Prophet ﷺ, you must seek out the leader of your time and know him in order to definitively conduct your affairs under his leadership.

As for those who believe in the Imamate as religious authority, they base themselves on this *ḥadīth* to emphasize that whoever wants to be of the faithful has to know the person of authority to learn his religion from him. After all, being faithful but deriving your faith from a source that is opposed to religion is the essence of pre-Islamic times.

We now come to those who raise the Imamate to the rank of moral guardianship. They interpret the *ḥadīth* to mean that the person who does not orient himself toward a perfect guardian will be like those who died a pre-Islamic death.

I mentioned this *ḥadīth* primarily for its recurrence (*tawātur*). I would like you to keep it in mind because we will return to it later.

Let us now move on to the verses of the Noble Qur'ān.

The Imamate in the Qurʾān

There are many verses in the Qurʾān that the Shīʿa have used to justify the Imamate. One of them is the verse: "Your guardian is only Allah."[26] What's important about all these verses is that the Sunnis have narrations related to them that support and confirm the view of the Shīʿa.

In the Qurʾān, there is the verse: "Your guardian is only Allah, His Prophet, and the faithful who maintain the prayer and give the *zakāt* while bowing down."[27] This "only" (*innamā*) in the verse signifies specification. The word *innamā* is an exceptional particle (*adāt ḥaṣr*). The primary meaning of *walī* is "the person most entitled (*awlā*) to act; the one most qualified to manage and command." This means that guardianship in the verse means to act and to manage.

The verse is saying, "Your guardian who is entitled to command you is only Allah ﷻ, the Prophet ﷺ, and the faithful who maintain the prayer and give alms while bowing down."

If we go back to the rulings of Islam, we won't find anything about the obligation (*wujūb*) of giving alms while bowing down. In other words, this is not a general ruling that includes everyone without exception and specification. This means that the verse is referring to an incident that actually happened; it is an incident that enjoys Sunni and Shīʿī consensus.

The summarized incident is this: a beggar went into the mosque while Imām ʿAlī ﵇ was praying. The Imām ﵇, who was wearing a

---

[26] Sūrat al-Māʾida, verse 55.

[27] Sūrat al-Māʾida, verse 55.

ring, extended his small finger, and the beggar took the ring and went on his way. Imām ʿAlī 🕮 didn't even wait to finish his prayers; he hastened to give his ring away. He pointed to it to make the beggar understand that he could take it and benefit from its price.

Among both the Sunnis and the Shīʿa, no one denies that Imām ʿAlī 🕮 gave his ring away mid-prayer and that the verse was revealed on his account. As we know, there are no rulings in Islam that make it obligatory or commendable (mustaḥabb) to make donations while bowing in prayer. For this reason, it may not be said that anyone other than Imām ʿAlī 🕮, who was specified by this verse, performed this deed.

The verse "and give the zakāt while bowing down"[28] signifies the man who did so during that well-known incident; it contains an allusion and a metonymy (kināya). As for using the plural to refer to a singular individual, this often occurs in the Qurʾān.[29]

This means that the verse appointed Imām ʿAlī 🕮 as a guardian of the ummah in terms of taking action, ruling, and commanding and forbidding.

The verse is also significant for other reasons that we will speak about later.

---

[28] Sūrat al-Māʾida, verse 55.

[29] [Arabic translator's note]: The plural form may be used to refer to the singular if it refers to someone great and lofty. Allah 🕮 says, "Indeed We have sent down the Reminder, and indeed We will preserve it" and "Had We wished We would have given every soul its guidance." Allah 🕮 also says: "Then stream out [afīḍū; plural] from where the people stream out" although He 🕮 is only speaking to the Prophet 🕮. There are many other examples. As this is certain, the verse "the faithful who maintain [yuqīmūn, plural] the prayer" could also refer to one person. See also, al-Tibyān fī tafsīr al-Qurʾān, Shaykh al-Ṭūsī, 3 (Maṭbaʿat Maktabat al-Iʿlām al-Islāmī), 562-63.

Other significant verses for our purposes are those revealed on the occasion of Ghadīr Khumm. The issue of al-Ghadīr itself is part of the Prophetic precept, and we will look into it later in the section entitled "The Imamate According to the Prophetic Precept." The verses revealed about this incident in Sūrat al-Māʾida include: "O Prophet! Communicate that which has been sent down to you from your Lord, and if you do not, you will not have communicated His message."[30]

The verse is so strongly-worded that it reflects the general meaning of the *ḥadīth*: "Whoever dies without knowing the Imām of his time will die a pre-Islamic death." The verse is telling the Prophet ﷺ that if he does not communicate what was revealed to him, he will not have communicated Allah's ﷻ message.

Both the Sunnis and the Shīʿa agree that Sūrat al-Māʾida was the last Sūra that was revealed to the Prophet ﷺ and that its verses were the last to be sent down to the him over his thirteen years in Mecca and ten years in Medina. This means that the content of these verses was among the last Islamic rulings and commands.

The Shīʿa pose this question: what is this thing that was among the last things to be sent down to the Prophet ﷺ? What's this thing that had such an importance that all the Prophet's ﷺ mission (*biʿtha*) would've been for nothing if he did not communicate it?

You [Sunnis] cannot point to an issue that took place during the last days of the Prophet ﷺ that was as important as his whole message such that if he did not communicate it, he wouldn't have communicated his message at all.

[30] Sūrat al-Māʾida, verse 67.

However, we Shīʿa can say that this issue is none other than the issue of the Imamate. Without the Imamate, everything would have been in vain. The very fabric of Islam wouldn't have held together; it would've fallen apart.

The Shīʿa use the narrations of Ahl al-Sunnah to support their belief that the verse was revealed about Ghadīr Khumm.

The noble verse "Today I have perfected your religion for you, and I have completed My blessing upon you, and I have approved Islam as your religion"[31] refers to that important incident which amounted to perfecting Allah's ﷻ religion and completing His ﷻ blessing on humanity. Because of this incident, Islam gained its meaning and became a religion that Allah ﷻ approves of. Without this incident, Islam would no longer be Islam; its meaning would not be what Allah ﷻ wanted it to be.

The Shīʿa base themselves on the verse's strong and emphatic language to infer the incident's importance. They wonder about the topic that could count as perfecting Allah's ﷻ religion and completing His ﷻ blessing. Its importance is equal to the importance of Islam itself because its absence means the absence of Islam.

The Shīʿa believe that they can specify and name this issue, but the Sunnis cannot say the same thing. In addition, there are narrations that assert that the verse was revealed about this specific incident.

Using these three verses, I gave an overview of the Shīʿa's proofs of the Imamate.

---

[31] Sūrat al-Māʾida, verse 3.

The Imamate and Clarifying Islam after the Prophet

In the previous chapter, I spoke of the Imamate and analyzed it from different angles. I emphasized that these different levels have to be distinguished or else we won't be able to look into the issue of the Imamate and analyze it properly.

I mentioned that one of the dimensions of the Imamate is the issue of rulership (*al-ḥukm*). The question is this: "What is the obligation (*taklīf*) toward the (Islamic) government after the passing of the Prophet (pbuh)? Will it be left to the *ummah*, assigning it the obligation of electing a ruler, or did the Prophet ﷺ himself appoint his successor?"

The issue has been phrased like this lately, and people have necessarily looked to the theory of Ahl al-Sunnah because it's the theory that seems the most intuitive to them.

Incorrect Propositions

People have been proposing the issue this way. Concerning the issue of government, what is the obligation toward rulership after the passing of the Prophet ﷺ? Is rulership hereditary or by designation (*tanṣīṣī*)? In the latter case, the current ruler would appoint his successor and specify him to the people without the *ummah*'s interference in the issue. This means that the Prophet ﷺ would appoint a ruler for the *ummah* after him, and this ruler would appoint his successor and so on until the Day of Judgment. In this case, the ruler is always chosen by appointment and designation.

In such a case, this "rule" would not necessarily be limited to the twelve Imāms (a) because the number of Imāms (a) in Shīʿī belief is twelve and only twelve. In contrast, this view supposes a general rule that dictates rulership in Islam. According to this rule, the Prophet ﷺ must appoint his successor, and that successor must appoint his successor, and so on until the Day of Judgment.

According to this view, rulership in Islam will remain controlled by this general rule even if Islam conquers the world. This has actually happened, as Islam now controls half the world and includes about seven million Muslims.[32] If Islamic rulings are to be followed by establishing one or multiple governments, that general rule would have to be followed.

If the Prophet ﷺ appointed ʿAlī ؑ as his successor, this may have been according to the general rule that states that ruling has to be by appointment and designation. Based on this view, the Prophet ﷺ did not have to appoint ʿAlī ؑ as a ruler after him in submission to the command of Allah ﷻ. This is because the Prophet ﷺ himself could explain things according to the revelation that he ؑ receives, and the Imāms ؑ after him can do the same because they are inspired (*mulhamūn*, sing. *mulham*) and because they receive their knowledge from the Prophet ﷺ. However, this does not apply to the rulers that would come after them.

This means that if rulership in Islam were based on designation and appointment, the Prophet ﷺ wouldn't have had to resort to divine revelation to appoint ʿAlī ؑ. The Prophet ﷺ could have appointed ʿAlī ؑ based on what he thought was right, and so could the Imāms ؑ. Each of them could have appointed his successor based on what they thought was best.

---

32 [Arabic translator's note]: This number corresponds to the number of Muslims in the world during the time of the author.

According to this logic, the issue of the Prophet ﷺ appointing ʿAlī ؑ as his successor is downgraded to an administrative level similar to appointing a governor over Mecca or choosing a manager over the pilgrims. No one says that the Prophet ﷺ appointed a governor of Mecca or sent Muʿādh b. Jabal to spread Islam in Yemen as a result of revelation. It could've have also been said that the Prophet ﷺ appointed ʿAlī ؑ as his successor out of his own accord because Allah ﷻ allowed the Prophet ﷺ to lead the *ummah* and manage society, and He ﷻ permitted him to act on his own judgment when he does not receive a specific revelation. His biography contains examples of this such as sending Muʿādh b. Jabal to Yemen and appointing a governor over Mecca.[33]

Presenting the Imamate according to this simple, naïve view that turns government into a worldly affair and that reduces Imamate to rulership has nothing to do with the form of the Imamate that we are discussing.

I repeat that if the Imamate were reduced to this level, there would be no need for revelation to interfere. The best revelation can do in such a case is to tell the Prophet ﷺ that it is his duty to elect whoever he sees fit as successor after him without designating a specific person. In this case, the Prophet ﷺ would choose according to what he thought was right, and his successor would choose his successor, and so on, until the Day of Judgment.

If we present the Imamate so naively, reducing it to rulership, and equating it to government, the theory of Ahl al-Sunnah would be more appealing than that of the Shīʿa.

---

33 [Arabic translator's note]: Based on this logic, the Imamate descends to the level of an ordinary administrative issue that is related to the governor's prerogatives. It relates in no way to the elevated view of the Imamate in Shīʿī belief, which encompasses clarification of Islam, guidance, and guardianship.

The Sunnis do not believe that the ruler is entitled to appoint his successor but that this is a job for the whole *ummah.* Influential people in society should hasten to assume this responsibility, and the ruler would be elected according to democratic principles. Choosing the ruler, for the Sunnis, is a right of the *ummah,* and the *ummah* should exercise its right of election.

However, the issue is not so simple. The designation of ʿAlī and the rest of the Imāms عليهم السلام is a secondary issue that is related to a much more important issue according to the Shīʿa.

The question that poses itself here is this: "The Imāms عليهم السلام are twelve in number, so what is the fate of Islamic rule after them?" Let us suppose that things went according to the Prophet's ﷺ directions, and rulership went to Imām ʿAlī عليه السلام, Imām al-Ḥasan عليه السلام, and Imām al-Ḥusayn عليه السلام down to Imām al-Ḥujja al-Mahdī عجل الله فرجه الشريف.

Let us suppose that Imām al-Mahdī عجل الله فرجه الشريف did not face circumstances that forced him to resort to occultation (*al-ghayba*) as we Shīʿa understand it. Let's suppose that he عليه السلام ruled after his father عليه السلام for a short period like his ancestors did and then passed away. What should be done with the matter of rulership then? Would the number of Imāms عليهم السلام exceed twelve? It would not. This means that the issue that is important for society is rulership in its ordinary, current state.

This conclusion comes up again but from another angle: we know that Imām al-Mahdī عجل الله فرجه الشريف cannot direct the affairs of the Muslims in occultation. This would cause the issue of the government and worldly rule to remain as it is.

Governing is a Branch of the Imamate

We must never commit the mistake of equating the issue of the Imamate in the Shīʿī context to governing and restricting it to rulership. Committing such a mistake makes the Imamate a simple and naïve issue that has consequent results.

When the Imamate is reduced to government, the main question that arises is: "Who is the person who should become the ruler? Should this ruler be the best of all his peers or should he be relatively better than them?"

Is it enough for him to be better than his peers at the level of management and politics despite being inferior to them on other levels? Is it enough for him to be a competent manager who doesn't cheat?

Other secondary questions also arise, such as: "Should this ruler be infallible or not? Why is infallibility necessary? Should he be committed to maintaining the night prayers (*ṣalāt al-layl*), and why is that necessary? Should he be knowledgeable about jurisprudence (*fiqh*) and the rulings of the Sharia and why or why not? Couldn't he consult other people in this regard and suffice himself with being relatively better than his peers?"

This form of the Imamate is limited to these questions, and it results mainly from the logic that equates the Imamate to government only and considers it a minor and marginal issue. This is a big mistake that some ancient theologians committed.

This mistake is frequently made today; as soon as the Imamate is mentioned, people think of governing although governing is only a minor, secondary component of the Imamate.

We should be careful not to confuse the Imamate and the issue of government. What is the Imamate then?

The Prophet's ﷺ Successor

The primary issue concerning the Imamate is succeeding the Prophet ﷺ in clarifying and explaining Islam without resorting to revelation, as the Imām ؑ does not receive revelation.

Without a doubt, only the noble Prophet ﷺ receives revelation. With his passing, revelation stopped and the message came to an end.

The primary issue concerning the Imamate may be formulated by the following question: can the task of clarifying the teachings of heaven be limited to one person and without the use of *ijtihād* and personal opinion? The *ummah* would refer to this person in religious matters as it had referred to the Prophet ﷺ, knowing that he speaks the truth which cannot be mixed up with personal opinions and ideas. In this case it cannot be said that this person may make a mistake and fix it the next day.

When we speak of the Prophet ﷺ, we do not say that he ever gave a wrong answer or deliberately acted according to his own whims. Such talk and ideas go against our understanding of the Imamate. If we know that certain words were definitively spoken by the Prophet ﷺ, we never say that he said them by mistake or due to inattention (*ghafla*).

This logic may apply to a *marja' al-taqlīd*; he might answer a question incorrectly or inattentively. The possibility of making mistakes, not paying attention, and being subject to certain influences applies to everyone except the Prophet ﷺ. In the same way, we can never say that the revelation was mistaken about a certain verse of the Qur'ān or that the revelation was unjust and subject to whims.

If the revelation makes a mistake concerning a verse, the verse in question would not be part of the revelation to begin with.

We return to our question. Is there a person after the Prophet ﷺ who is an authority when it comes to the rulings of Islam? Does a perfect person with such qualifications exist?

I already mentioned that such a person exists. The only difference is that the words of the Prophet ﷺ are a direct result of the revelation whereas the words of the Imāms عليهم السلام are based on the Prophet ﷺ and not on revelation. It cannot be said that the knowledge that the Imāms عليهم السلام received from the Prophet ﷺ were taught to them directly by him. Rather, their knowledge can be explained based on Imām 'Alī's عليه السلام saying, "The Prophet ﷺ taught me a thousand doors of knowledge, and every door led to a thousand other doors."[34]

We can't entirely explain that, just like we can't explain the nature of revelation and the way that the Prophet ﷺ received his knowledge from Allah ﷻ. We cannot explain the spiritual connection that was between the Prophet ﷺ and 'Alī عليه السلام such that the Prophet ﷺ was able to teach Imām 'Alī عليه السلام the complete truth as it truly was.

---

[34] [Arabic translator's note]: al-Irshād cites 'Abdullāh b. Mas'ūd as saying, "The Prophet of Allah called for 'Alī and they had a private conversation. When 'Alī came back out to us, we asked him, 'What did the Prophet tell you?' He said, "He taught me a thousand doors of knowledge, and every door opened up a thousand doors before me." Al-Irshād, 1/34. Ahl al-Sunnah narrate that 'Alī said, "The Prophet of Allah taught me a thousand doors of knowledge, and every door included a thousand doors." See Farā'id al-simṭayn, 1/101 and Yanābī' al-mawadda, 1/83.

In *Nahj al-Balāgha,* Imām ʿAlī ﷷ speaks about accompanying the Prophet ﷺ to the cave of Ḥirāʾ when he was a boy. Imām ʿAlī ﷷ says that he heard a whine when revelation came to the Prophet ﷺ, so he asked, "O Prophet of Allah, what was that sound?" The Prophet ﷺ said, "That was Satan. He has despaired from being worshipped ever again. You see what I see and hear what I hear but you are not a prophet."[35] Similar words often appear in other sources.

If someone else were next to ʿAlī ﷷ at the time, he wouldn't have heard that sound. This is because the sound that Imām ʿAlī ﷷ heard wasn't a physical sound that everyone could hear; the incident speaks of another kind of hearing and sight.

The Imāms' ﷷ Infallibility

The spiritual aspect relates primarily to the Imamate. The word "Imāms" refers to spiritual human beings who are beneath the rank of the Prophet ﷺ but who know Islam and practice it by a spiritual way. The Imāms ﷷ, like the Prophet ﷺ, are infallible and cannot make mistakes, become inattentive, or commit sins.

The Imām ﷷ represents a certain, definitive authority such that if we heard him say something, we would never think that it contains error or deliberate deviation. This is what infallibility means. A *ḥadīth* that the Shīʿa often narrate from the Prophet ﷺ goes as follows: "I am leaving among you the notable two (*al-thaqalayn*), the Book of Allah and my family."

The first question that comes up here is this: "Did the Prophet ﷺ say this *ḥadīth* or not?"

---

[35] Nahj al-Balāgha, sermon 192.

This is an undeniable *ḥadīth* because the Shīʿa were not the only ones who narrated it; the Sunnis narrated it and recorded it in their books more than the Shīʿa did. I remember my first days in Qum; the journal *Risālat al-Islām,* published by Dār al-Taqrīb in Cairo, was still new, and a Sunni scholar cited the *ḥadīth* in an article of his, but it was like this: "I am leaving among you the notable two, the Book of Allah and my *sunnah* ." Sayyid Borujerdi ﵀, who was a real, high-minded scholar, asked Shaykh Qavām Vishnoi to track the *ḥadīth* in the books of Ahl al-Sunnah. Shaykh Qavām was a diligent student who read a lot and was known for his accuracy. The Shaykh accepted his task and the result of his research was that two hundred books of Ahl al-Sunnah actually narrate the *ḥadīth* using the formula: "I am leaving among you the notable two (*al-thaqalayn*), the Book of Allah and my family."[36]

The Prophet ﷺ uttered the *ḥadīth* in this form on many occasions, but that does not mean that he never said, "I am leaving among you the notable two, the Book of Allah and my precept." The Qurʾān, the precept, and the Prophet's family ﵈ are not contradictory elements; the Prophet's family ﵈ explains the Prophetic *sunnah* .

The matter is not limited to two choices for us to ask, "Should we go back to the precept or to the Prophet's family ﵈?" The question is not whether we should go back to one or the other but whether the Prophet's family ﵈ has the actual explanation of the precept and know it fully. The meaning of "the Book of Allah and my family" is that we must learn the sunnah from the Prophet's family ﵈.

Besides, the saying, "I am leaving among you the notable two, the Book of Allah and my family" is itself a part of the Prophetic *sunnah*

[36] Saḥīḥ Muslim, 7/122.

because it is a *ḥadīth.* This means that there is no contradiction here.

In addition, the Prophet ﷺ uttered the *ḥadīth,* "I am leaving among you the notable two, the Book of Allah and my *sunnah* " once, and it is not a definitive *ḥadīth,* whereas he uttered the first formulation, "the Book of Allah and my family" many of times. The second formulation appears in one book but two hundred books have recorded the *ḥadīth* in its original formulation ending with "and my family."

Shaykh Qavām Vishnoi sent the treatise that he wrote at Sayyid Borujerdi's ؒ directions to Dār al-Taqrīb in Egypt. The publishing house was fair and unbiased in its reaction to the treatise, printing and publishing it after realizing its scholarly nature that could not be denied or criticized.

If the late Ayatollah Borujerdi ؒ wanted to behave like some people do, his reaction would've been limited to making a racket and saying, "What do these people want? They're denying the rights of Ahl al-Bayt ؑ and are full of bad intentions." However, because he chose the high road, Shiʿism achieved a great thing by having the treatise published in Cairo.

What we have discussed so far is that the authentic Imamate is a result of Islam being a comprehensive, universal, and eternal religion. The question that arises here is this: "Does Islam only equal the principles and generalities mentioned in the Qurʾān and the words of the Prophet according to the narrations of Ahl al-Sunna?" In other words, do these two sources contain all the aspects of Islam?

Of course, Islam was completely revealed to the Prophet ﷺ. However, the question is whether the Islam that the Prophet explained and promulgated is equal to the Islam that was revealed to him ﷺ. Were many Islamic matters left unexplained although Islam itself was completely revealed to the Prophet ﷺ because its contexts hadn't emerged yet? These matters needed time to unfold, and the knowledge of them rested with ʿAlī ؑ who later explained them to the people.[37]

This is the primary issue of the Imamate.

The *ḥadīth* "the Book of Allah and my family" also implies infallibility because the Prophet ﷺ is urging the *ummah* to learn its religion from these two sources: the Book and the Prophet's family ؑ. Just as the Qur'ān is infallible, the second source also has to be infallible. It's impossible for the Prophet ﷺ to call people to learn their religion from this source so decisively if this source commits mistakes.

At this point precisely, the theories of the Sunnis and the Shīʿa go their separate ways about the explanation and teaching of religion. The Sunni theory says that just as the revelation ceased with the death of the Prophet ﷺ, the actual explanation of Islam that is infallible and not subject to confusion stopped too. There is nothing beyond our inferences about the Qur'ān and the *ḥadīths* of the Prophet ﷺ. This is knowledge of Islam in its perfect form.

[37] [Arabic translator's note]: Perhaps this text clarifies the author's meaning of the duty of Imām ʿAlī and the rest of the Imāms ؑ. The Prophet ﷺ said to ʿAlī ؑ in one of his instructions to him, "Tell the people my words and explain things to them after I am gone." ʿAlī asked, "O Prophet of Allah, did you not communicate all that was entrusted to you?" The Prophet said, "I did, but you will explain things to them when they disagree about them after me." See *al-Irshād*, 1/46.

Forbidding the Recording of Ḥadīths

However, a certain incident took place that is related to the Sunnis and that weakens their theory. ʿUmar forbade the recording and writing of the Prophet's *ḥadīths.*

This is a historical incident. Let me forget that I am a Shīʿa scholar who has his own position. Let me pretend to be a European Orientalist who is not bound by belonging to either the Shīʿa or the Sunnis. The best this orientalist can say without ill intentions is that ʿUmar acted like this out of his conviction that the Qurʾān is the only reference since he said, "The Book of Allah is sufficient for us." In other words, he forbade the *ummah* from studying the science of *ḥadīth* and writing it down because relying excessively on *ḥadīth* weakens the *ummah*'s reliance on the Qurʾān.

This incident, as I mentioned, is a historical fact that is not limited to us Shīʿa. In ʿUmar's time, no one dared to write *ḥadīth*s down and no one dared to transmit *ḥadīth*s from the Prophet ﷺ. The transmission of *ḥadīth* was forbidden. This prohibition continued until the days of ʿUmar b. ʿAbd al-Azīz who was caliph for three years (r. 99-101 AH). During his time, this precept of ʿUmar was disregarded and *ḥadīth* was written down again.

The people who had memorized *ḥadīth* from one generation to another then narrated the *ḥadīths* that they knew and they were recorded and written down. This state of affairs led to the loss of a part of the Prophet's ﷺ *ḥadīths.*

If we examine the issue from another angle, the rulings of the Qurʾān are very concise and general. The Qurʾān contains generalities. For example, despite its great insistence on prayer, the

Qur'ān only tells us, "Maintain the prayer"[38] and speaks of bowing in general without mentioning the details of performing the prayer. The same thing applies to the obligation of performing the pilgrimage. The Qur'ān doesn't detail any of the acts of pilgrimage that the Prophet ﷺ performed.

The Prophetic *sunnah* also follows this general, concise formula. Even if it wasn't so concise, how long did the Prophet ﷺ have to demonstrate what was permissible (*ḥalāl*) and impermissible (*ḥarām*)? During his thirteen years in Mecca, the number of Muslims didn't exceed four hundred Muslims at most, and it was a time of siege and pressure too. During such circumstances, the Muslims could only meet the Prophet ﷺ secretly, not to mention that seventy families—about half or more of the total number of Muslims—immigrated to Abyssinia (*al-Ḥabasha*).

This was the Prophet's ﷺ reality in Mecca; it only afforded few opportunities. Although things were better in Medina, the Prophet ﷺ had many troubles there too.

Let us disregard the realities of Mecca and Medina and suppose that the Prophet's ﷺ only care across those twenty-three years was to teach the people. Even in such a case, that time would not enough for the Prophet ﷺ to explain all the components of Islam. What if that time was also consumed by the incidents of actual history that took up most of the Prophet's ﷺ time, particularly since Islam is a religion that encompasses all the aspects of human life?

[38] Sūrat al-Baqara, verse 43.

Analogical Reasoning

This logic of Ahl al-Sunnah caused them to find glaring practical gaps in the rulings of Islam. Whenever an issue comes up for which there is no legal ruling in the Qur'ān, they resort to the *sunnah* —as little of it as they transmitted—where they also find nothing.

In such a case, can the issue be left without a ruling? If the answer is no, what should be done? Their answer to this question is analogical reasoning. Analogical reasoning means looking for similarities between things that have rulings in the Qur'ān or the *sunnah* and things that do not. If two issues were similar, the issue without a ruling would be viewed analogously to the issue that has a ruling and would receive the same treatment.

As an example, if it is thought that a certain ruling came from the Prophet ﷺ for a certain reason, whenever this reason comes up, the same ruling would apply based on speculation.

These gaps were not one or two; the Islamic world was expanding, particularly during the time of the Abbasids. Lands were conquered, and new needs came up that raised new questions. When the supporters of analogical reasoning looked to the Qur'ān and the *sunnah* , they didn't find answers for the issues they were facing. That's why they resorted to analogical reasoning. Despite this, Ahl al-Sunnah split into two groups on this issue. The first group refused analogical reasoning, like Aḥmad b. Ḥanbal and Mālik b. Anas. It is said that Mālik resorted to analogical reasoning only twice throughout his life. The second group practiced analogical reasoning extensively, even excessively, like Abū Ḥanīfa. Abū Ḥanīfa did not believe that the *sunnah* that people are familiar with actually came from the Prophet ﷺ. It was even said that he only counted fifteen Prophetic *ḥadīths* as trustworthy. In such a case, it's only natural that he filled the gaps using analogical reasoning.

As for al-Shāfiʿī, he took the middle way between the two groups: he relied on *ḥadīth* in some instances and on analogical reasoning in others.

This led to the emergence of an astonishing form of jurisprudence.

It was said in this regard that Abū Ḥanīfa relied so heavily on analogical reasoning because he was a Persian—Persians were known to prefer rational matters—and because he lived in Iraq, far from Medina, the heartland of the traditionalists (Ahl-al-Ḥadīth).

Abū Ḥanīfa practiced analogical reasoning heavily and he let his imagination run wild in this domain. Ahl al-Sunnah themselves had even recorded the following incident. Abū Ḥanīfa went to the barber one day. His hair was just starting to turn white. He asked his barber to remove the white hairs so they wouldn't increase, but the barber told him that white hairs increase when they are removed. Based on this, Abū Ḥanīfa asked his barber to remove his black hairs. This request of his was a result of analogical reasoning that went as follows: If white hairs increase and grow when they are removed, then black hairs should increase and grow when they are removed too. This was although the rule applied to white hair only.

This was how Abū Ḥanīfa practiced jurisprudence.

The Shīʿa and Analogical Reasoning

When we go back to the narrations of the Shīʿa, we realize that they demolish this kind of thinking entirely by showing how mistaken is the idea that the Qurʾān and the *sunnah* aren't enough.

Relying on analogical reasoning goes back to the assumption that the Qur'ān and the *sunnah* aren't enough to clarify legal rulings. Saying that the Qur'ān and the *sunnah* aren't enough leads to analogical reasoning.

However, what we have from the generalities of the Prophetic *sunnah* either directly from the Prophet ﷺ himself or indirectly from his trustees عليهم السلام spares us the trouble of resorting to analogical reasoning.

This is the spirit of the Imamate from the religious perspective. Islam isn't simply a trend for the creator of this trend to say, after his ideology emerges, that this trend needs a form of government. No, Islam is a religion, an eternal and comprehensive religion.

No Need for Election

We now come to the Imamate in its dimension of political leadership and government. When the Prophet ﷺ names his successor, and this successor is an Imām who is infallible like the Prophet, elections and consultations and so on become meaningless. Anyone named by the Prophet ﷺ is above the rest and even has exceptional prerogatives just like the Prophet ﷺ.

During the Prophet's time ﷺ, he was never asked who would assume control of the government. No one claimed that the Prophet's ﷺ only duty was to receive the revelation whereas the duty of the government depended on consultation or the *ummah*'s opinion, which would determine if the Prophet ﷺ or someone else would rule. The same thing applies to the Prophet's legatees. In the presence of the Prophet ﷺ, who rises above the world of mortals thanks to his connection to the revelation, such issues don't come up. They shouldn't come up after the Prophet ﷺ either, as he has twelve trustees whose duty, over more than two centuries, has been to strengthen the pillars of Islam. In this case, Islam would be explained through a pure, unerring fountain of knowledge.

With such an authority that explains the rulings of Islam, it's pointless to talk about the form of rulership and whether it should take place through election and consultation. In the presence of an infallible person who has perfect knowledge and who does not even get confused, is it right to disregard him and elect someone else?

In addition, appointing ʿAlī ﷺ as Imām in the meaning that we have been discussing necessarily means that he would also assume political leadership. Political leadership is a characteristic of the Imām and the Imamate, and the Prophet ﷺ declared that ʿAlī ﷺ is entitled to this position.

Let us be very careful here, however. The Prophet ﷺ made this declaration about ʿAlī's ﷺ right to rulership and political leadership because ʿAlī ﷺ fulfilled all the other requirements of the Imamate.

Yes, during the occultation of Imām al-Mahdī ﷺ, when the infallible Imām is not in control, the matter of rulership takes a different form. We can present the issue in another way. Let's assume that the things that happened during the formative years of Islam did not happen and that Imām ʿAlī ﷺ became the Prophet's ﷺ successor without interruption, and then he was succeeded by Imām al-Ḥasan ﷺ and Imām al-Ḥusayn ﷺ down to Imām al-Ḥujja al-Mahdī ﷺ. Let us assume that Imām al-Mahdī ﷺ did not face circumstances that forced him to resort to occultation but that his life was like the life of his fathers before him. After the *ummah* would be left without his infallible presence ﷺ, the issue of rulership would take a different form. At that point we would have to ask: "What should be done about the issue of rulership? Should the ruler be the jurist who fulfills all the requirements or is that not necessary? Should the *ummah* elect the ruler?"

For this reason, the issue of the Imamate should not be discussed as a marginal worldly issue that is reduced to rulership from the start. We should not base questions on this premise such as: "Is rulership in Islam by appointment or election? What do the Shīʿa say about such a theory of rulership?"

The issue isn't actually like this. The Shīʿī theory is that of the Imamate. Rulership is one of the duties of the Imām. Naturally, no other person should be suggested for this position in the presence of the infallible Imām. This was the case during the time of the noble Prophet ﷺ; the rulership of anyone else in his presence is unthinkable. The Prophet ﷺ appointed ʿAlī ؑ as the Imām, and the Imamate entails rulership.

In addition, the Prophet announced the rulership of ʿAlī ؑ on different occasions, but this announcement came in the form of "the Imām after me is ʿAlī." If ʿAlī ؑ is the Imām, he is the ruler too.

Moral Guardianship

In our previous session, [in the previous chapter], I briefly spoke of an idea that I personally believe in and consider central. It is not counted among the pillars of Shīʿism, however. This idea is expressed by the following questions: is the position of the noble Prophet ﷺ limited to receiving the divine rulings and the principles and branches of Islam through revelation? Is his ؑ knowledge limited to knowing Islam at the practical level without being informed of anything else by Allah ﷻ? Was the Prophet ﷺ infallible at the level of acts and piety?

Concerning the Imāms عليهم السلام, were their positions limited to receiving Islam through the Prophet ﷺ—as they did not receive revelation—such that their knowledge of the generalities, particularities, and branches of Islam was like the knowledge of the Prophet ﷺ, not subject to error and confusion? Were they infallible at the level of piety and acts too? Are there other forms of knowledge that the Prophet and the Imām عليه السلام know? What do they know aside from the affairs and the sciences of religion?

Is it true that the acts of people are presented to the Prophet ﷺ and to every Imām عليه السلام in his own time such that Imām al-Mahdī عجل الله تعالى فرجه الشريف now does not only observe the Shīʿa but all people?

In this form of guardianship, there is no difference whether the Imām عليه السلام is alive or dead. Like I already said, when you visit Imām ʿAlī b. Mūsā al-Riḍā عليه السلام, you address him with the words: "Peace be upon you." You will be in a state of witnessing (*shuhūdiyya*), as when you speak to a living person and say to him, "Peace be upon you."

This is called moral guardianship.

In the previous session, I mentioned that this idea is a common point between Shīʿism and Islamic mysticism (*ʿirfān*). The ideas of the two schools are very similar. The mystics believe in the necessity of the existence of the Pole and the Perfect Man in every age. The Shīʿa also believe in the existence of the Imām عليه السلام in every age; no time is without an Imām and a Proof who is the Perfect Man.

At the moment, I don't want to discuss the topic of moral guardianship because there is no disagreement about it between us and the Sunnis. The difference between us and them is in the first two ranks, i.e. the Imamate that means explaining religion and the Imamate that means political leadership.

Ḥadīth al-Thaqalayn

We must pay attention to the Imamate entailed in the *ḥadīth*: "I am leaving among you the notable two (*al-thaqalayn*)." If you ever debate with a Sunni person, whether he is a scholar or not, ask him whether this *ḥadīth* came from the Prophet ﷺ or not. If he says that it did not, you can refer him to a number of Sunni books that mentioned it.

The scholars of Ahl al-Sunnah cannot disagree with us about the soundness (*ṣiḥḥa*) of this *ḥadīth*.[39]

Ask any person about the meaning of the Prophet's ﷺ family. Why did he insist that people use the Qur'ān and his family as references? Ask the Sunnis why they don't differentiate between the Prophet's ﷺ family and others? Why do they focus on the transmission of *ḥadīths* on the differentiation between companions and non-companions? Why do they narrate fewer *ḥadīths* from ʿAlī ؑ than from other people? When they do narrate from ʿAlī ؑ, why do they treat him like any other narrator and not as an authority and reference?

---

[39] This *ḥadīth* suffered at the hands of some preachers of 'Āshūrā' and reciters of the *taʿziya* because they used it as a preface to discussing the calamity that took place. One would think that what the Prophet ﷺ meant by leaving behind the Qur'ān and his family ؑ was that the *ummah* only had to respect these two elements and not wrong them. However, the Prophet ﷺ actually wanted the *ummah* to refer to both of these two authorities at the same time: the Qur'ān and his family ؑ. The Prophet ﷺ wanted the *ummah* to hold fast to these two authorities and never let go of them. This is implied by the rest of the *ḥadīth*: "if you hold fast to them, you will never go astray." The point of the *ḥadīth* is the authority of both elements. The Prophet ﷺ considered his family ؑ the equivalent of the Qur'ān when he called on people to refer to them. The Prophet ﷺ also said, "The Qur'ān is the greater load (*al-thiql al-akbar*) and my family is the lesser load (*al-thiql al-aṣghar*).

Ḥadīth al-Ghadīr

We mentioned that the person who is a reference in religious matters also has to be the religious and political leader. The Prophet ﷺ declared Imām ʿAlī's ﵇ leadership through *ḥadīth* al-Ghadīr, which the Prophet ﷺ uttered on the occasion of the farewell pilgrimage at Ghadīr Khumm.[40]

The farewell pilgrimage was the last pilgrimage that the Prophet ﷺ went on. After the conquest of Mecca, the Prophet ﷺ only went on pilgrimage once, although performed the ʿ*umra* before he went on the farewell pilgrimage.

The Prophet ﷺ called on the people to go on pilgrimage to Mecca with him, so they gathered and went. He ﵇ gave sermons in various places along the way: al-Masjid al-Ḥaram, ʿArafāt, Minā, just outside of Minā, at Ghadīr Khumm, and in other places.

One of the places where the Prophet ﷺ gave a sermon was Ghadīr Khumm; it was the last and most intense sermon. I personally think that the Prophet ﷺ had a philosophy behind delaying this sermon which goes back to the verse: "O Prophet! Communicate that which has been sent down to you from your Lord, and if you do not, you

---

40 [Arabic translator's note]: This distinction between the Imām's duties as an authority and explainer of religious matters and as a political and social leader of the *ummah* was clarified by Shahīd Sayyid Muḥammad Bāqir al-Ṣadr. Shahīd al-Ṣadr wrote about Imām ʿAlī's ﵇ role in Islam, saying, "The Prophet did not appoint ʿAlī as a supreme authority after him only at the social level but on both the social and intellectual levels. Imām ʿAlī was given two kinds of authority by Allah ﷻ and the Prophet. The first is the social authority that gave Imām ʿAlī actual leadership of the Muslims in their social life. The second is the intellectual and legislative authority that made the Imām the primary reference after the book of Allah and the precept of His Prophet regarding Islam's rulings, legislations, values, and concepts. The greatest Prophetic expression of the first kind of authority was *ḥadīth* al-Ghadīr while the greatest expression of the second kind of authority was *ḥadīth al-thaqalayn*." From a review that Shahīd al-Ṣadr wrote to the book *Musnad al-Imām ʿAlī* by Sayyid Ḥasan Gubbanchi in the *Qaḍāyā Islāmiyya*, 3 (1417 AH): 631.

will not have communicated His message."[41] After the Prophet ﷺ communicated the generalities of Islam in its principles and branches in his sermons at ʿArafāt, Minā, and al-Masjid al-Ḥaram, he ﷺ received an order from heaven to communicate a specific thing. If he ﷺ didn't communicate this specific thing, it would be as though he did not communicate the message at all: "if you do not, you will not have communicated His message."[42] This means that if he had communicated everything except this one thing, all his work would have been in vain.

It was then that the Prophet ﷺ asked the gathered crowd, "Don't I have a greater authority over you than you have over your own selves?" This was a reference to Allah's ﷻ saying, "The Prophet has a greater authority over the faithful than they have over their own selves."[43] What he meant was, "Am I not more entitled than you to manage your own affairs?"

Everyone without exception responded, "Indeed, O Prophet of Allah." The Prophet then said, "Whoever accepts me as his master (*mawlā*), ʿAlī is his master." This *ḥadīth*, like *ḥadīth al-thaqalayn*, has many chains of transmission (*asānīd*, sing. *isnād*).

Muʾassasat Nashr al-Ḥaqāʾiq al-Islāmiyya in Mashhad published a research on the occasion of al-Ghadīr a few years ago. I haven't had the chance to read this work so far, but some expert colleagues of mine have read it and praised it as very good. I recommend that you at least read this work.

---

[41] Sūrat Māʾida, verse 67.

[42] Sūrat Māʾida, verse 67.

[43] Sūrat al-Aḥzāb, verse 6.

As Shīʿa, we believe that *ḥadīth* al-Ghadīr is recurrent (*mutawātir*). If we want to investigate the sources in which it appears, it would take us a very long time. This also applies to *ḥadīth al-thaqalayn,* to which Sayyid Mīr Ḥāmid Ḥusayn—the author of *ʿAbaqāt al-anwār*—dedicated a big book of four-hundred pages within his encyclopedia.

Perhaps the topic requires further discussion, but I have favored limiting myself to the essence of the matter of the Imamate while making general references to the Shīʿa's proofs of it.

A Theological Discussion of the Imamate

To better understand Shīʿa scholars' logic on the Imamate, as well as others' opinions on it, I chose to present to you what Khoja Naṣīr al-Dīn al-Ṭūsī said about the issue, with clarifications whenever necessary.

Shaykh al-Ṭūsī's words are very brief, and they have been discussed among Sunni and Shīʿa scholars from his time until today.

Shaykh al-Ṭūsī wrote a book entitled *al-Tajrīd*; you must've heard of it. A section of the book discusses the art of logic; it's entitled "The Logic of *al-Tajrīd.*" The second section is on the art of theology (*kalām*), discussing the issues of monotheism, prophethood, the Imamate, and the Day of Return, among other issues. The section on monotheism is predominantly philosophical, as the Shaykh used the philosophers' methodology in that section.

Al-ʿAllāma al-Ḥillī explained both sections of the book. You must've heard of ʿAllāma al-Ḥillī; he's one of Islam's major jurists. The Shīʿa aren't alone in regarding him as a great jurist: he is considered a great jurist in Islam generally.

Al-ʿAllāma al-Ḥillī was Shaykh al-Ṭūsī's student in logic, theology, philosophy, and mathematics, and al-Muḥaqqiq al-Ḥillī's student in jurisprudence. Al-Muḥaqqiq al-Ḥillī is the author of *Sharāʾiʿ al-Islām*, and he is also an eminent jurist of the Shīʿa.

Al-ʿAllāma and the Khoja were both considered geniuses. Khoja Naṣīr al-Dīn al-Ṭūsī is a world-class mathematician. The papers recently mentioned that some lunar craters have been named after a number of Iranian mathematicians, such as the Omar Khayyam crater, the Nasireddin crater, and the Avicenna crater. Khoja Naṣīr al-Dīn al-Ṭūsī had a number of scientific theories about the moon.

Al-ʿAllāma al-Ḥillī was a genius in jurisprudence. He wrote many books and compilations in the field such as his two-volume *Tadhkirat al-fuqahāʾ*. Truth be told, when one reads this book, he is amazed at the mastery of one individual person.

Although *Tadhkirat al-fuqahāʾ* is a jurisprudential book, it is not limited to the jurisprudence of the Shīʿa. It includes the legal opinions (*fatāwā*; sing. *fatwa*) of all the scholars of Ahl al-Sunna, not only their four Imāms, i.e. Abū Ḥanīfa, al-Shāfiʿī, Mālik, and Aḥmad. The book mentions the opinions of other great jurists without limiting the jurisprudential schools to four. When discussing legal rulings, Khoja Naṣīr al-Dīn al-Ṭūsī presents the opinions of Abū Ḥanīfa, al-Shāfiʿī, and the other Sunni scholars before mentioning the Imāmīs' legal ruling.

In addition, al-ʿAllāma al-Ḥillī mentions that a jurist has had multiple opinions on a topic. He mentions, for instance, that al-Shāfiʿī had this opinion the first time and another one later. He also mentions his own opinion then says that he changed his mind.

In this regard, Shaykh Muḥammad Taqī al-Qummī mentions that when the *Tadhkira* was going to be published, the publishing house sent for Sunni scholars who were specialists in every Sunni legal school. When these scholars arrived, they were amazed that al-ʿAllāma al-Ḥillī was more knowledgeable about Sunni opinions than they were. This was al-ʿAllāma al-Ḥillī; he was an exceptional man.

Al-ʿAllāma al-Ḥillī wrote a commentary on *al-Tajrīd.* The commentary on the section on logic came to be known as *al-Jawhar al-naḍīd*, which is one of the most important books on logic. The commentary on the theological section was entitled *Khashf al-murād*, and it is now known as *Sharḥ al-Tajrīd.*

Al-ʿAllāma al-Ḥillī's commentary on both sections was characterized by brevity. Al-ʿAllāma's commentary was explained many times after him, and many glosses (*ḥawāshī*, sing. *ḥāshiya*) were written about it. The commentators on it split into criticizers and defenders. Perhaps no book in the whole Islamic world enjoyed the same level of discussion and analysis as *al-Tajrīd.* Many commentaries and glosses to it were written, either agreeing or disagreeing with its author. The reason for this is Khoja's method in writing *al-Tajrīd*: when he wanted to discuss the Shīʿī view of things, he was very brief. He wrote his book as brief texts that contained certain ideas that he passed over quickly.

Toward the end of *al-Tajrīd*, Khoja al-Ṭūsī wrote a discussion of the Imamate. Since his discussion is accepted by all the scholars of the Shīʿa, his overview gives us a glimpse of Shīʿī scholars' logic about the Imamate.

The book I'm holding right now is Mullā ʿAlī al-Qūshjī's commentary on *al-Tajrīd.* Mullā al-Qūshjī is an eminent Sunni scholar. His position, which is naturally opposed to Khoja al-Ṭūsī's, led him to defend the theories of Ahl al-Sunnah and respond to Khoja Naṣīr al-Dīn often.

For this reason, this commentary came to reflect the Shīʿī scholars' theories and views about the Imamate as reflected in Khoja Naṣīr al-Dīn's words as well as the theories of Ahl al-Sunnah.

The Definition of the Imamate

Any discussion of the Imamate should begin with a definition of it. There does not seem to be a disagreement about the definition, which is as follows: "The Imamate is general leadership in the matters of religion and this world."

Shaykh al-Ṭūsī used a theological term when he said, "The Imām is a manifestation of grace (lutf)." What he means is that the Imamate is a counterpart of prophethood: it falls outside the choice and ability of human beings, and it is connected to another source that it came from. If prophethood comes from revelation and is a heavenly appointment, the Imamate—prophethood's counterpart—comes through appointment by the Prophet ﷺ in obedience to Allah ﷻ. The difference between the two is that prophethood comes from Allah ﷻ directly, and the Prophet ﷺ is connected to Him directly. As for the Imām ؈, the Prophet ﷺ appoints him in obedience to Allah ﷻ.

The Shīʿa's Rational Proof of the Imamate

Khoja al-Ṭūsī's words in this regard did not exceed one sentence. [44]The commentaries of Shīʿī scholars on it follow the basis that I spoke of earlier. The scholars of the Shīʿa base themselves on the discussion of history. They believe that the main topic is the Imamate of ʿAlī b. Abī Ṭālib ؈; if they can prove his Imamate, the Imamate of the other Imāms ؈ follows by designation. This deductive logic of the Shīʿī scholars is based on the premise that Islam is a universal religion that encompasses all the affairs of

---

44 [Arabic translator's note]: This is the sentence: "The Imām is a grace, and it is necessary for Allah to appoint him in order to achieve His purposes." See Kashf al-murād fī sharḥ Tajrīd al-iʿtiqād (Muʾassasat al-Nashr al-Islāmī al-Tābiʿa li-Jamāʿat al-Mudarrisīn, Qum, 1407 AH), 362.

human life. The reality of this religion reflects this, as it has a say in all matters of life.

As a second step, the Shīʿa pause at the Prophet's ﷺ biography and ask, "Does the Prophet's ﷺ biography indicate that he had a sufficient chance to teach the people Islam fully despite all its broadness?"

History indicates that the Prophet ﷺ did not have such a chance during the twenty-three years of his mission.

The Prophet ﷺ obviously made use of all available chances, and he ﷺ taught the Muslims many Islamic rulings. However, the details of his life in Mecca and Medina, with all of its problems and concerns meant that this period was not enough for him to teach all the Muslims all the rulings.

The third step of this proof is that it is impossible for this religion to have been left deficient. For this reason, a group or at least one person among the companions must have received Islam fully from the Prophet ﷺ and understood it completely. This student or group was then ready to explain Islam after the Prophet ﷺ like he used to explain it himself. The only difference is that the explanation of the Prophet ﷺ came directly from revelation, whereas the Prophet's successor undertook his mission because of the things that he learned from the Prophet ﷺ.

In the fourth step, Shīʿa scholars say that Ahl al-Sunnah did not have such a person [Imām/religious authority] to refer back to. They dealt with Islam as a deficient religion—whether they admit it or not—which eventually led them to come up with analogical reasoning.

Reality testifies to this. Analogical reasoning emerged for Ahl al-Sunnah when new issues that needed answers and rulings came up. When they considered these issues, they realized that the Prophet ﷺ didn't say anything about them, so they wondered what they should do.

The only solution they had was to make one issue analogous to another, relying on speculative similarity (*al-tashābuh al-ẓannī*) in the derivation (*istinbāṭ*) of rulings.

Although religion was assumed to be deficient and in need of analogical reasoning to be completed, the scholars of the Shīʿa never followed such a logic. In *Nahj al-Balāgha,* ʿAlī b. Abī Ṭālib ؑ denounced this logic and refused it, and the Imāms ؑ after him did the same. In this regard, Imām ʿAlī ؑ said, "Did Allah reveal a deficient religion" that He needed their opinions to complete it?

The Imāms ؑ stressed the fact that the issue is not an issue of deficiency, which requires filling the gaps using our opinions and speculations. There is a chapter in *al-Kāfī,* for instance, whose message is that the Qurʾān and the *sunnah* discussed everything that is permissible and impermissible, if only generally. The general features of all issues were included in the Qurʾān and the *sunnah* . The only thing that has to be done is uncovering their specific meaning.

Ijtihād in the Shīʿī view is nothing more than this. *Ijtihād* means the sufficiency of the generalities of Islam and its principles. The *mujtahid* only has to apply these general principles to the particularities in order to reach the desired rulings.

Analogical reasoning is different. Those who resort to analogical reasoning do not believe that these general principles are enough.

This is why they chase after similarities, speculation, and intuition to derive rulings in a speculative way.

We conclude from the above that the logic of the scholars of the Shīʿa is as follows: you and us [Shīʿī and Sunni scholars] agree that the noble Prophet ﷺ did not have the chance to explain all the rulings of Islam to the people throughout twenty-three years. Beyond that point, however, we disagree. You say that the Prophet ﷺ just left the *ummah* without consideration and passed away. We believe that the same proof of the Prophet's ﷺ mission proves that he ﷺ appointed certain people who had a holy aspect about them to succeed him.

The Prophet ﷺ took it upon himself to fully teach the first of these successors, i.e. Imām ʿAlī ؑ, all the truths of Islam so that he could answer all the questions that were directed to him. ʿAlī ؑ constantly urged the members of the *ummah* to ask him about anything that they wanted to know.[45]

The Imām: The Specialist in Islam

I would like to convey the idea through modern terminology. Shīʿī scholars say that people who deny the existence of an Imām with such characteristics are actually belittling Islam. Logically and intuitively, a specialist should accompany any apparatus when it is

---

[45] [Arabic translator's note]: In his sermons, ʿAlī ؑ urged the *ummah* to ask him questions to the point that he said, "O people, I am your Prophet's cousin, and the closest of you to Allah and His Prophet; ask me and ask me again." See *al-Irshād*, 1/229. In another sermon, he ؑ said, "Ask me before you lose me. By Allah, if you ask me about a group that will misguide a hundred and guide a hundred, I will tell you the identity of its leader on the Day of Resurrection." A man stood up and said, "Then tell me the number of hairs on my head and in my beard." See *al-Irshād*, 1/330. Most historical sources relate, through sound and multiple chains of transmission, that ʿAlī ؑ urged the *ummah* to ask him questions. See *al-Ghadīr*, 6/193-94, 7/107-08. The best statement of all, however, was mentioned in Aḥmad b. Ḥanbal's *Musnad*: "No companion of the Prophet used to say, 'Ask me before you lose me' except ʿAlī b. Abī Ṭālib." See *al-Ṣawāʿiq al-muḥriqa*, 76; *al-Riyāḍ al-naḍira*, 2/118.

sent somewhere. When a country like the U.S. or the USSR exports sophisticated machinery such as the Phantom or the MiG to a country that is not familiar with such machines, an accompanying specialist is sent along. Things differ when you are exporting something simple like textiles; you won't need a specialist. The question that I put to you is this: "How would you rate Islam, which came from Allah? Would you equate it to simple products like textiles, which don't need to be accompanied by a specialist when they are exported from one country to another or would you treat Islam like a complex technical apparatus that needs to be accompanied by a specialist?"

The Imām is actually a specialist in the matters of religion. He is a true expert, as his knowledge is never subject to mistake or confusion.

The noble Prophet ﷺ brought Islam to the people. This religion requires the presence of a divine authority to explain it to people completely, at least for a certain time. The Prophet ﷺ actually appointed such a specialist.

Shīʿī scholars express this necessary obligation by the term grace. They mean by it divine grace because the object of grace, i.e. the

Imamate, is beneficial to the guidance of humanity.[46] Since people cannot know the way, divine grace necessitates that Allah ﷻ should care for them. This also applies to prophethood, which is also governed by the rule of grace.

This rule is a Shīʿī principle. It may be said that this rule basically reflects the Shīʿa's rational proof of the Imamate.

---

[46] [Arabic translator's note]: They say that grace is anything that draws the servant closer to obedience and distances him from disobedience. Both prophethood and the Imamate are necessary divine graces, as they achieve the purpose behind creating humankind. Grace is of three kinds, depending on its source. It either comes from a subject, being Allah ﷻ or the accountable subject (*al-mukallaf*), or from an object. If grace comes from Allah ﷻ, it is necessary, as if He does not do it, it would oppose His purpose, which is something abominable and impossible. If grace comes from the accountable subject, Allah ﷻ should make this subject feel and know grace first. If it comes from an object that is neither Allah ﷻ nor His servants, the condition for making it obligatory is the knowledge of the accountable subject of it. An example of this is prayer. Prayer is obligatory, but this obligation depended on the Prophet ﷺ explaining it and the accountable subject performing it after learning about it from the Prophet ﷺ. For this reason, the sending of the Prophet ﷺ was necessary for Allah ﷻ, and explanation was required from the Prophet ﷺ. Commanding the servant to pray depends on this servant's knowledge that the Prophet ﷺ explained how to pray. That's when prayer becomes obligatory. All of this is due to the grace of Allah ﷻ. The rule of grace applies to the Imamate exactly like it applies to prophethood. The need for prophets is identical to the need for successors and trustees. Just as Allah ﷻ sent the prophets to guide people away from error, He appointed Imāms for that same purpose. It is known that the Shīʿa and the majority of the Muʿtazila believe in the necessity of grace, unlike the Ashʿarīs. See ʿAlī Muqallid, *Niẓām al-ḥukm fil-Islām* (Dār al-Aḍwāʾ, Beirut, 1406 AH), 273, 47-8, 35. See also *Kashf al-murād*, 362 (Qum: Muʾassasat al-Nashr al-Islāmī, 1407 AH).

Infallibility

At this point, the issue of infallibility comes up. When the Shīʿa view the Imām[47] as a protector and guardian of the Sharia and an authority for the *ummah*, what they mean is that the Imām ﷺ is infallible just like the Prophet ﷺ is infallible.

No one questions the Prophet's ﷺ infallibility; it's obvious. Anything that definitively comes to us from the Prophet ﷺ is not subject to doubt or confusion but is necessarily correct. The person sent by Allah ﷻ as a guide for people when they need divine guidance cannot err or sin.

Error is of two kinds. The first is when sin happens deliberately, such as if Allah ﷻ commanded the Prophet ﷺ to do something but the Prophet ﷺ decided to do it in a different way that opposed Allah's ﷻ original command.

Such a thing clearly goes against the meaning of prophethood.

If we define the Imamate as a complement of religion in the domain of explaining religion, this means that the Imamate is necessary for the Prophet ﷺ to do his duty of explaining the rulings

[47] This means that the Shīʿa place greater importance on the Imām's religious dimension, i.e. on the religious authority of his mission. We already mentioned that it's incorrect to equate the Imamate with government like some people in our own time do. As soon as the Imamate is mentioned, they immediately equate it to government. In other words, the issue is regarded from its worldly dimension. There is partial overlap (*ʿumūm wa khusūs min wajh*) between the Imamate and government. The Imamate is one thing, and government, which is a branch of the Imamate, is another. During the age of occultation, we speak of government but not the Imamate, which means we should not equate the Imamate to government. The Imamate, in the words of the scholars of theology, is leadership in religion and this world. Because it is leadership in religion, it is necessarily leadership in this world too. The Prophet ﷺ himself was like this. Since the Prophet ﷺ is a leader in religion, he is consequently a leader in the world. If the Imām was not present in a certain age, or if he was in occultation, such that the position of religious leadership was empty, then we ask about religious leadership and wonder about the obligation concerning it.

of religion. In this case, the same proofs for the infallibility of the Prophet ﷺ apply to the Imām ﵇.

If some will object by saying that the Imām ﵇ does not have to be infallible because there are other people to correct him if he makes mistakes, we respond by applying this logic infinitely to all these other people. The impossibility of infinite regress (*burhān al-taṭbīq*) leads us to the necessity of an infallible person who safeguards the Sharia.[48]

If we suppose that the Imām may make mistakes or sin, others would be obligated to criticize him for it, which contradicts the command to obey him. These two things are opposites that cannot coexist.

---

[48] [Arabic translator's note]: In the words of Naṣīr al-Dīn al-Ṭūsī, "the impossibility of infinite regress necessitates the Imām's infallibility, in addition to his being the preserver of the Sharia. The Imām would be condemned if he sinned and countered the command of obedience, thwarting the purpose of his appointment. If he were not infallible, he would be demeaned in the eyes of the lowest members of the masses." In mentioning these reasons that necessitate The Imām's infallibility, al-Ṭūsī commits to his methodology of brevity. This makes it necessary to go back to al-ʿAllāma al-Ḥillī who expands these reasons by saying this. First, if the Imām were not infallible, this would necessitate infinite regress, which is impossible. The explanation of this conditional sentence is this: the reason for the necessity of appointing the Imām is that his subjects may err. Therefore, if this reason applied to the Imām, he would need an Imām himself in a chain of regression that must end in an Imām who does not err and who is the real Imām. Second, the Imām is the preserver of the Sharia so he has to be infallible. Al-ʿAllāma al-Ḥillī explains this by saying that the Sharia is not preserved by the Qurʾān, the precept, the consensus of the *ummah* (*al-ijmāʿ*), governorship, or fundamental license (*al-barāʾa al-aṣliyya*). This leaves only the Imām as a preserver. If the Imām could make mistakes, we could no longer trust the obligations and acts of worship imposed by Allah ﷻ. This contradicts the purpose of obligation, which is submission to Allah ﷻ. If the Imām makes mistakes, it would be obligatory to criticize him for it, which contradicts the command of obeying him: "Obey Allah and obey the Prophet and those vested with authority among you." If the Imām sins, this would contradict the purpose of appointing him. The purpose of appointing him is the *ummah*'s submission to him and to his orders and following his example. If he sins, this would cancel all these obligations, which contradicts the purpose of appointing him. If the Imām sins, this would put him beneath the rank of the masses because his intellect is better and his knowledge of Allah ﷻ and His rewards and punishments is greater than that of the masses. This means that if he sins, he would be beneath his subjects. All of this necessarily cannot be. See *Kashf al-murād*, 364-65 (paraphrased).

Designation

From infallibility we can prove the issue of designation. The theological argument for the case, which begins with Allah ﷻ, is as follows. The Imamate is a grace from Allah ﷻ, and His grace is necessary (*wājib*). Since this grace is incomplete without infallibility, the Imām ؑ has to be infallible. For this same reason, he has to be expressly designated, because infallibility cannot be determined by the people.[49]

Knowing and determining the Prophet ﷺ is not left to the people. Allah ﷻ appoints the Prophet ﷺ and makes him known to the people through proofs, signs, and miracles. For this reason, the people have nothing to do with determining and appointing the Imām ؑ. The Imām ؑ also has to be appointed by Allah ﷻ. The difference between the Prophet ﷺ and the Imām ؑ is that the people recognize the Prophet's ؑ prophethood through signs and miracles without the interference of any human being. The Imamate, in contrast, is made known through a human, i.e. the Prophet ﷺ.

At this point, the proof moves on to designation. The Imamate, in the meaning we have been discussing, has to be by the Prophet's ؑ appointment and not by the designation of the people.

---

[49] Naṣīr al-Dīn al-Ṭūsī expresses this aspect of the Imamate in his succinct way by saying, "Infallibility necessitates designation, and the Prophet's way of doing things also necessitates designation." Al-ʿAllāma al-Ḥillī explained this on two levels. 1- The Imām has to be infallible, and infallibility is a hidden aspect that only Allah ﷻ knows. This means that the designation of the Imām has to come from Allah ﷻ because He alone knows the conditions of infallibility. 2- Al-ʿAllāma al-Ḥillī based himself in this point on the Prophet's ؑ care for his *ummah*; he ؑ is more compassionate toward it than a father toward his child. He ؑ did not neglect even minor issues that concern it, so how can he be accused of neglecting his *ummah* and not guiding it in the most important and beneficial of matters? This matter refers to the identity of his ؑ successor. The Prophet's ؑ way of doing things then necessitates appointing the Imām after him, designating him, and introducing him to the people. Al-ʿAllāma al-Ḥillī then adds, "This is a reasoned fact (*burhān limmī*)." See *Kashf al-murād*, 366-67.

We can see that the proof progressed from grace to infallibility, and then moved from infallibility to designation.

When the proof gets to this point of demonstration, we come to the fourth step that is summarized in the following question. Let us assume this is all true, but what does this have to do with ʿAlī ﵇? Khoja Naṣīr al-Dīn answers us, "These two characteristics are specific to ʿAlī." He means that infallibility and designation are specific to ʿAlī ﵇.

His point is that no one disagrees about the fact that only ʿAlī ﵇ was designated. The issue is not that they claim that the Prophet ﷺ designated someone else while we say that he ﵇ designated ʿAlī ﵇. No. The issue rather revolves around this question: did the Prophet ﷺ appoint and designate someone or did he not designate anyone at all? If we answer that he did designate someone, this only applies to ʿAlī ﵇.[50]

This means that if we believe that designation is necessary and that the Prophet ﷺ did designate someone, this designated person can only be ʿAlī ﵇. No one else ever claimed to be designated; the concept of designation itself was refused. The caliphs themselves did not claim that they were designated, and neither did other people. None of their followers claimed that they were designated either.

This proves our premise.

---

[50] [Arabic translator's note]: Again we return to al-ʿAllāma al-Ḥillī as he explains Naṣīr al-Dīn al-Ṭūsī's meaning: "Infallibility and designation are specific to ʿAlī. There are two opinions in the *ummah*: those who do not believe in infallibility and designation and those who do. I have already proved the falsity of the first opinion, which means that the second opinion is true." Elsewhere he says that all those who believe in infallibility and designation have said that the Imām is ʿAlī ﵇. This may be explained by saying that those who say that designation is necessary unanimously agree that ʿAlī is the infallible person who was specified by designation. See *Kashf al-murād*, 367 (paraphrased). See also ʿAlī Muqallid, *Niẓām al-ḥukm fil-Islām*, 390.

The same proof applies exactly to the issue of infallibility. None of the caliphs claimed that they were infallible. They frankly admitted their mistakes. None of the Ahl al-Sunnah say that they were infallible either because the Imamate for them only means government. According to Sunni logic, it is meaningless to talk about the ruler being infallible and free of mistakes in the domain of government. The ruler makes a lot of mistakes and even sins, but he is an upright person who is eligible to lead the prayer.

This is what the Sunnis say. Their definition of the ruler does not exceed this. For this reason, Ahl al-Sunna—and Mullā al-Qūshjī agree with them—narrate that Abū Bakr said, "There is a devil that takes hold of me," and he willingly said: "If I deviate, set me straight."[51]

Some of those who recorded 'Umar's words in this regard claimed that he said them on seventy different occasions. No one denies their frequency and the agreement of the Sunnis and the Shī'as about them. He said many different times, "'Umar would have been doomed without 'Alī." Sometimes he made mistaken judgments. Imām 'Alī ﷺ corrected him, and 'Umar himself accepted these corrections.

This means that the caliphs neither claimed infallibility for themselves nor had others claim it on their behalf.

When the Imamate is presented so loftily and is based on grace, infallibility, and designation, no one will claim that anyone other than 'Alī ﷺ was eligible.

---

51 [Arabic translator's note]: *al-Ṣawā'iq*, 7; *al-Imāma wal-siyāsa*, 1/2; *Sharḥ Nahj al-Balāgha*, 2/8.

This is the theological discussion of the Imamate, which is, like I mentioned, a top-down discussion. It proves the necessity of the Imamate using the same proofs for the necessity of prophethood because the Imamate is also a manifestation of grace. Since divine grace is necessary, the Imamate is necessary too.

It seems that it is possible to conclude the discussion of the Imamate here, but let's discuss it further to see if reality on the ground agrees with the results of the theoretical theological discussion. Did the Prophet ﷺ designate ʿAlī ؑ or did he not? Approaching the topic from this angle allows us to consider its textual aspect.

Before we begin with the textual discussion, I would like to discuss the idea contained in the question of some people: "Why do we follow a top down approach in the theological discussion of the Imamate? We better begin from the bottom, meaning from actual reality."

The theologians usually began from the top down to reach this conclusion. Proceeding from the opposite direction, the theologians' question about whether the Imamate is a divine grace or not becomes irrelevant.

Those who object to the top-down approach say that it basically means assigning an obligation to Allah ﷻ, with all the theological components of obligation. In other words, the Imamate is a manifestation of grace, and grace is necessary for Allah ﷻ, so He must appoint the Imām. They do no not want to enforce an obligation on Allah ﷻ, believing that they should look to reality. If the Prophet ﷺ designated someone, that is enough for them without investigating the implications of the Imamate being a grace, including the proof of infallibility and designation rationally.

Let's look to the Prophet ﷺ: did he appoint someone as Imam or not?

We should investigate the proofs of the Shīʿa that are part of the down-top approach. It is best to do so briefly, as Ahl al-Sunnah mostly don't believe in these texts. I don't mean that they absolutely deny them, but they consider them non-recurrent and belonging to the category of singular report (*khabar wāḥid*). If they do accept these texts, they interpret them in a different way than we do.

A Textual Investigation of ʿAlī's Imamate

It is stated that the noble Prophet ﷺ said to his companions, "Salute ʿAlī as the Commander of the Believers."[52] This saying is related to the occasion of al-Ghadīr.

The famous sentence in *ḥadīth* al-Ghadīr: "Whoever accepts me as his master, ʿAlī is his master," is narrated separately. The Sunnis do not consider this a recurrent Prophetic *ḥadīth* and they do not believe that the Prophet ﷺ said, "Salute ʿAlī as the Commander of the Believers."

The scholars of the Shīʿa strove to prove the recurrence of such *ḥadīths*. In his *al-Tajrīd*, Naṣīr al-Dīn al-Ṭūsī accepts this *ḥadīth* without further comment, whereas the commentator Mullā ʿAlī al-Qūshjī objects by saying that they as Sunnis do not accept this *ḥadīth* as recurrent. He says that they consider it a singular report that is narrated without unanimity.

---

52 [Arabic translator's note]: After the occasion of al-Ghadīr, ʿUmar turned to ʿAlī and said, "O ʿAlī, you are now the master of every faithful man and woman." See *Rawḍat al-aḥbāb*, 416. Ibn Ḥajar says in his *Ṣawāʿiq*, "Two Bedouins came forth with a disagreement and ʿUmar let ʿAlī judge between of them. One of the Bedouins complained: 'He judge between us?!' ʿUmar indignantly rose up and grabbed the collars of the speaker's garment, saying, "Watch it! Don't you know who this man is? This is my master and the master of every faithful person. Those who refuse him as a master are not faithful." See *al-Ṣawāʿiq*, 179.

The authors of encyclopedic works such as *al-Ghadīr* and *al-ʿAbaqāt* made every effort to prove the *ḥadīth*'s recurrence. These two encyclopedias, and *al-Ghadīr* particularly, trace the narrators and transmitters of the *ḥadīth* through every generation of Muslims from the first to the fourteenth century in the sources of Ahl al-Sunnah. According to these books, the narrators of the *ḥadīth* included over sixty companions. After the companions, the authors moved on to the generation of the followers (*al-tābiʿūn*) who heard the *ḥadīth* from the companions. These two generations are practically limited to the first Hijri century.

The narrators of the *ḥadīth* were then traced across the centuries from one generation to another. The author of *al-Ghadīr* did a fine job when he made use of literary works in his endeavor. Other books, like *al-ʿAbaqāt,* limited themselves to transmitting the *ḥadīth* and mentioning its narrators in every century. *Al-Ghadīr,* on the other hand, paid attention to the literary dimension because the poetry of every era reflects its concerns and depicts the happenings of the poets' times.

The logic of the book is that if the incident of al-Ghadīr were a construct of the fourth Hijri century, it wouldn't have appeared in poetical works of the first, second, and third century since every century included poets that recited verses about al-Ghadīr. Based on this logic, how can this *ḥadīth* be denied?

This is a fine methodology in historical research. Literature is often used to prove certain historical matters. If we noticed that literary writers generally discussed an idea, we would be certain that this idea is a historical truth.

The author of *al-ʿAbaqāt* followed a different methodology based on writing extensively. For example, he might write a whole book about one *ḥadīth,* mentioning all of its narrators and judging their trustworthiness as transmitters.

The author of this book uses his investigative methodology to build a marvelous edifice around the *ḥadīths* that he discusses. His research abilities are astounding.

Another piece of textual evidence for ʿAlī's Imamate is the Prophet's ﷺ saying to him, "You are the successor after me."

There are more examples of textual evidence, but unfortunately, I lost my notes while I was leaving our gathering[53] a couple of weeks ago. These notes contained the *ḥadīths* relevant to the Imamate. Of course, I still know the sources that contained these *ḥadīths,* but I cannot remember the details.

Of the *sīra* works that go back to the second Hijri century is the *Sīra* of Ibn Hishām. Ibn Hishām seems to have lived in the third Hijri century,[54] but the bulk of his *Sīra* goes back to Ibn Isḥāq[55] who lived in the early second century. The latter's *Sīra* ended up in the hands of Ibn Hishām who summarized and arranged it.

Ibn Hishām *Sīra* is very important for Ahl al-Sunnah. The book mentions two incidents that are not included in *al-Tajrīd,* but I will allude to them because they are similar to other textual examples in this regard.

---

[53] [Arabic translator's note]: These lectures on the Imamate were given in the Muslim Physicians' Union.

[54] [Arabic translator's note]: Ibn Hishām died in the year 218 AH.

[55] [Arabic translator's note]: Muḥammad b. Isḥāq died around the year 152 AH.

The Day of the Warning

The first incident is related to the early days of the Prophet's ﷺ mission when the verse: "Warn the nearest of your kinsfolk"[56] was revealed. The Prophet ﷺ hadn't publicly declared his mission yet, and ʿAlī ؑ was still a young boy who was living in the Prophet's ﷺ own home. ʿAlī ؑ lived with the Prophet ﷺ from his childhood, but that is a story for another time. The Prophet ﷺ called for ʿAlī b. Abī Ṭālib ؑ and said to him, "O ʿAlī, Allah ordered me to warn my nearest kinsfolk. Prepare an amount of food and gather Banū Hāshim and Banū ʿAbd al-Muṭṭalib for me." ʿAlī ؑ prepared the meal, which consisted of mutton and milk to drink. After the attendees ate and had their fill, the Prophet ﷺ wanted to speak, but Abū Lahab intercepted him and said, "How has he enchanted you all!" This made everyone leave and the Prophet ﷺ did not have the chance to talk to them.

The Prophet ﷺ told ʿAlī ؑ to prepare food again and gather the people the following day. ʿAlī ؑ, the narrator of this report, did so. He says in this regard, "I did as I was told and then I invited the people like the Prophet asked. There were about forty men. After they all ate and had their fill, the Prophet spoke to them and said, 'By Allah, I do not know of any Arab youth who brought to his people something better than what I am bringing you. I have brought you the good of this world and the Hereafter, and Allah has ordered me to call you to Him. Which one among you will assist me in this and in return be my brother, legatee, and successor among you?"

Everyone kept silent except ʿAlī ؑ. The Prophet ﷺ repeated his question, and the same thing happened again. The Prophet ﷺ put

---

[56] Sūrat al-Shuʿarāʾ, verse 214.

his hand on the back of ʿAlī's ﷺ neck and said, "This is my brother, legatee, and successor among you."

With the Tribal Leader

The other incident in the *Sīra* of Ibn Hishām happened to the noble Prophet ﷺ while he was still in Mecca when Quraysh was still hurting him and preventing him from communicating his message. The Prophet ﷺ benefited from the pilgrimage season because Quraysh used to give up harming him throughout the sacred months (*al-ashhur al-ḥurum*);[57] it would refrain from physically harming the Prophet ﷺ while continuing its propaganda against him.

During this season, the tribes gathered at the market of ʿUqāẓ, which was near ʿArafāt. The goal of the gathering was performing the pilgrimage but in a different way than we're used to. The Prophet ﷺ used to make use of this chance to present himself to the tribes and call them to Islam. Meanwhile, Abū Lahab followed him everywhere like his own shadow, accusing him of lying and trying to prevent him from reaching out to people.

During one pilgrimage season, the Prophet ﷺ happened to speak to a certain tribal leader who was gifted in physiognomy (*firāsa*). After speaking with the Prophet ﷺ for a short time, he said, "By Allah, if I could take this youth from Quraysh to my side, I would vanquish all the Arabs through him." The man then turned to the Prophet ﷺ and asked, "If we pledge allegiance to you and Allah grants you

---

[57] Wars were suspended in Dhū al-Qiʿda, Dhū al-Ḥijja, and Muḥarram because they were sacred months. During these months, the tribes refrained from acts of revenge. People walked without fear and all the tribes safely gathered in the market of ʿUqāẓ. Even if someone saw the murderer of his own father, he would do him no harm out of respect for the sacred months.

victory over those who oppose you, will we be in control after you?" The Prophet ﷺ responded, "Allah does as He wills."

The incident shows that that tribe's faith was not true. The Prophet ﷺ was clear in saying that the appointment of his successor is not up to him but to Allah ﷻ. This incident is mentioned in the books of Ahl al-Sunnah.[58]

The Concurrence of Ḥadīth al-Ghadīr

Another text that the Shīʿa use as proof is *ḥadīth* al-Ghadīr. In *al-Tajrīd*, Khoja Naṣīr al-Dīn says, "As for the recurrent *ḥadīth* al-Ghadīr..."

In the terminology of the science of *ḥadīth* (*ʿilm al-ḥadīth*) there are the terms "recurrent report" (*khabar mutawātir*) and "singular report" (*khabar wāḥid*). Singular report means the report that is transmitted by one person or the report whose transmission does not inspire certainty (*yaqīn*), regardless of whether it has been transmitted by one person or ten.

As for the recurrent report, it is the report that is transmitted by a group of people whose number excludes the possibility of conspiring to lie. To clarify this, if a person said that he heard a certain piece of news on the radio, you would suspect that it's true, but you would still wait to see what other people were saying. If you heard the same news from another person, your certainty about it would increase. If it was reported by many people at once, it would not be possible to say that they were all lying.

---

58 [Arabic translator's note]: Ibn Hishām, *al-Sīra*, 2/66: "The Prophet presents himself to Banū ʿĀmir b. Ṣaʿṣaʿa."

The number of transmitters should get to a point where they could not be suspected of conspiring to lie; at a certain number, it may be assumed that a group of transmitters have conspired together to lie. However, beyond a certain number, conspiracy is no longer possible.

To go back to the example of the radio, it is possible for ten people to conspire to lie and tell false news. Even a hundred people may do so. However, the number might reach a point where the possibility of conspiring to lie is no longer possible. If you go to south Tehran and hear the news, then hear a group talking about it in east and west Tehran as well, you can no longer suspect that all these people conspired together to lie.

Such a report is called a recurrent report.

The Shīʿa believe that the transmitters of *ḥadīth* al-Ghadīr reached a number that they cannot have conspired to lie. It cannot be said that forty companions of the Prophet ﷺ agreed to transmit a false report, especially since some of the *ḥadīth*'s transmitters were enemies of ʿAlī ؑ or, in the very least, they weren't of his supporters.

If all the transmitters of *ḥadīth* al-Ghadīr were like Salmān, Abū Dharr, and al-Miqdād—i.e. figures who were followers of ʿAlī ؑ—they might have agreed to transmit such a *ḥadīth* due to their close relationship to ʿAlī ؑ. However, some of the *ḥadīth*'s transmitters were not connected to ʿAlī ؑ and did not favor him, so such a proposition is invalid.

The point of disagreement is that people like Mullā ʿAlī al-Qūshjī say that *ḥadīth* al-Ghadīr is a singular, non-recurrent report, whereas the Shī'a say that the *ḥadīth* is recurrent and cite books written on the topic as proof.

In *ḥadīth* al-Ghadīr, we read that the Prophet ﷺ asked, "Don't I have a greater authority over you than you have over your own selves?"[59] They said, "Indeed." The Prophet ﷺ then said, "Whoever accepts me as his master, 'Alī is his master." The Prophet ﷺ clearly wanted to give 'Alī ؑ the same mastery that he himself had over people, based on the verse: "The Prophet has a greater authority over the faithful than they have over their own selves."[60]

Ḥadīth al-Manzila

Another *ḥadīth* that Khoja al-Ṭūsī uses as proof and classifies as recurrent is *ḥadīth al-manzila*. Whereas al-Ṭūsī holds that the *ḥadīth* is recurrent, Mullā 'Alī al-Qūshjī insists that it is a singular report. Mullā al-Qūshjī does not deny the *ḥadīth*; he only denies its recurrence.

Some scholars who dedicated themselves to this *ḥadīth* include Mīr Ḥāmid Ḥusayn in his *al-'Abaqāt* and al-Amīnī in *al-Ghadīr*. Mīr Ḥāmid Ḥusayn dedicated an entire volume of his *al-'Abaqāt* to *ḥadīth al-manzila*. In contrast, al-Amīnī did not focus on other *ḥadīths* as much as he focused on *ḥadīth* al-Ghadīr.

---

[59] This is a reference to Allah's ﷻ saying, "The Prophet has a greater authority over the faithful than they have over their own selves" (Sūrat al-Aḥzāb, verse 6). According to the verse, since the Prophet ﷺ is sent by Allah ﷻ, he has authority over people, their possessions, and their other domains of authority. His ﷺ authority over people's domains of authority is greater than their own. Every person in society has authority over his money, self, and the rest of his affairs, but the Prophet's ﷺ authority is even greater. Obviously, the Prophet ﷺ never practiced this authority for his own benefit; he is a deputy (*wakīl*) appointed by Allah ﷻ over society. If a person has the authority and right to do as he wishes with his own self and money for his own benefit, the Prophet ﷺ has greater prerogatives that serve the interests of Islamic society as a whole.

[60] Sūrat al-Aḥzāb, verse 6.

In *ḥadīth al-manzila*, the Prophet ﷺ told ʿAlī ؑ, "Your position from me is like Hārūn's position from Mūsā except that there is no prophet after me." The Prophet ﷺ said this to ʿAlī ؑ as he ؑ was setting off for the Expedition of Tabūk. There was no fighting in the Expedition of Tabūk; it was an act of mobilization that the Prophet ﷺ initiated and that ended without fighting after the Byzantine army withdrew from the area. This expedition, which was named after the area of Tabūk to the north of Medina, took place after the Expedition of Muʾta. The Expedition of Muʾta is considered the first and only battle between the Arabs and Byzantium during the time of the Prophet ﷺ.

Constantinople, present-day Istanbul, was the capital of the Byzantine Empire. Syria was part of this empire. The Byzantines were preparing to mount an attack on Medina from Syria, so the Prophet ﷺ thought it was of in Islam's best interests to march with an army to the Byzantine border.[61]

The Prophet's ؑ goal, in political terms, was to display his power and announce his readiness for battle. He ؑ led his army to the borders of Byzantium and went back to Medina. The Prophet ﷺ did not take ʿAlī ؑ on this expedition but left him as his second in command in Medina. Shīʿī scholars explained this step as a consequence of the Prophet's ؑ knowledge that no fighting will take place. Imām ʿAlī ؑ was upset at having to stay behind in Medina with the women and children. This is because the hypocrites told lies claiming that the Prophet ﷺ left him behind because he found him burdensome. ʿAlī ؑ caught up with the

[61] [Arabic translator's note]: Last year, I went to Khaybar. I had no idea that the distance from Khaybar to Medina and from Medina to Tabūk was so long! The distance from Medina to Tabūk in a straight line was a hundred parasangs or six-hundred kilometers. Perhaps it was even longer in the past due to the crooked nature of the roads back then. The distance between Medina and Khaybar was sixty parasangs. It made me wonder at the high spirits that allowed the Prophet ﷺ and the Muslims to travel such distances using the means of transportation of their time.

Prophet at al-Jurf on the outskirts of Medina to tell him what the hypocrites were saying, and the Prophet ﷺ told him, "Wouldn't you be content to have your position from me [or: Your position from me is] like Hārūn's position from Mūsā except that there is no prophet after me?"[62]

This *ḥadīth* means that everything that Hārūn ‎ had in relation to Mūsā ‎ except prophethood was accorded to ʿAlī ‎. Let's go back to the Qurʾān to see Hārūn ‎ position from Mūsā ‎. The Qurʾān cites prophet Mūsā ‎ as saying, "My Lord! Open my chest for me. Make my affair easy for me. Remove the hitch from my tongue, [so that] they may understand my discourse."[63] The verse that concerns us is the subsequent verse: "Appoint for me a minister [*wazīr*] from my family."[64] A *wazīr* originally meant a helper, and a *wizr* is a heavy weight. The meaning is that Mūsā ‎ wanted Hārūn ‎ to relieve him of some of the weight. Later, the term *wazīr* acquired the familiar meaning of a king's assistant.

Mūsā ‎ did not restrict himself to making this request; he suggested his brother by name. He said, "Hārūn, my brother. Strengthen my back through him, and make him my associate in my affair, so that we may glorify You greatly, and remember You greatly."[65]

---

[62] [Arabic translator's note]: See *Ṣaḥīḥ al-Bukhārī*, 4/24, 5/3; *Ṣaḥīḥ Muslim*, 4/187; *Jāmiʿ al-Uṣūl*, 8/649; *Maṣābīḥ al-Sunna*, 4/170; *al-Ṣawāʿiq*, 121; *al-Istīʿāb* (annexed to *al-Iṣāba*), 3/41. The Prophet ﷺ designated ʿAlī ‎ in *al-Bukhārī*, 5/3: "The Prophet of Allah ﷺ went out to Tabūk and left ʿAlī in command. ʿAlī said, 'Are you leaving me behind among the women and children?' The Prophet ﷺ said, "Wouldn't you be content to have your position from me like Hārūn's position from Mūsā except that there is no prophet after me?"

[63] Sūrat Ṭā Hā, verses 25-28.

[64] Sūrat Ṭā Hā, verse 29.

[65] Sūrat Ṭā Hā, verses 30-34.

In another place in the Book of Allah, we read Mūsā's saying to Hārūn: "Be my successor among my people."[66] For this reason, when the Prophet told ʿAlī, "Your position from me is like Hārūn's position from Mūsā" he meant all of Hārūn's attributes in the Qurʾān—being a minister, associate, and successor—except prophethood.

If the phrase "except that there is no prophet after me" wasn't included, it might've been said that the Prophet meant one specific similarity between ʿAlī and Hārūn. However, when the Prophet excluded prophethood, he was including all other affairs. Of course, this means social and not biological affairs; the Prophet did not mean that ʿAlī became his biological brother! The Prophet's meaning was that ʿAlī was like Hārūn with respect to Mūsā.

The response of Ahl al-Sunnah is that they are ready to accept this *ḥadīth* if it were recurrent but it is only a singular report.

However, like I already mentioned, scholars like Mīr Ḥāmid Ḥusayn proved the recurrence of *ḥadīth al-manzila.*

Audience Q and A

Question: The conclusion that I made based on last time's session and today's session is this. In my mind, there is a dividing line that separates the Imamate and the government based on Shaykh Muṭahharī's saying that the Imamate has many duties and branches, one of which is government. The question that occurred to me is this: what are the branches that cannot be attended to through

[66] Sūrat al-Aʿrāf, verse 142. The remainder of the verse is: "And Mūsā said to Hārūn, his brother, 'Be my successor among my people, and set things right and do not follow the way of the agents of corruption.'"

government alone? What we have learned from Islam so far is that it isn't a religion that separates this world and the Hereafter. Deeds that are related to the Hereafter are actually a guarantee of engaging with this world and a motivation for participating in this life. The aim of our deeds in this life is to achieve perfection and a better social life based on the establishment of social government.

When we go back to the Book of Allah, we find that it gives the highest accolades to servants who use their deeds to establish justice in the government of this worldly life. This is why it gives *jihād* the highest importance.

Looking back at the Imāms' عليهم السلام lives, their way of life and all their teachings are based on guaranteeing rights and gaining the right to dominion (*al-ḥākimiyya*) and rulership. There is no difference in this regard between the Imāms عليهم السلام who publicly waged *jihād* and the Imāms عليهم السلام who suffered imprisonment or established secret underground movements.

This reality makes me unable to imagine duties of the Imamate other than government: all the duties and the affairs of the Imamate can be included in and directed by the domain of rulership. What I mean is that the Imāms' عليهم السلام rule, when they finally get the change to rule, will become an organizing framework for all the duties and the branches of the Imamate. What I would like is a clarification of this issue.

Answer: I would like to point out at first that the concept of a dividing line came from the esteemed asker. I have personally never used such a term and I think it is incorrect to do so.

What I did say is that the Imamate is presented among the Shīʿa at a higher level than that of rulership and government. Rulership here is one aspect of the Imamate, and the layer that I spoke about was the Imām's ﷺ duty is to clarify Islam and act as an infallible authority in religious rulings that does not make mistakes.

In our logic we say that rulership is one of the affairs of the noble Prophet ﷺ; there is no dividing line between this world and the Hereafter that makes prophethood an affair of the Hereafter and rulership an affair of this world.

We say that one of the Prophet's ﷺ duties in the *ummah* is rulership, but this duty was not given to him ﷺ by the *ummah* as a right. Rather, it is a right that was given to him ﷺ by Allah ﷻ because he ﷺ is a human being who is above the mortal world due to his connection to the world of the unseen.

In other words, since the Prophet ﷺ is an explainer of divine rulings who has a spiritual connection to the world of the unseen, he must rule the *ummah*.

I did not mean to establish a dividing line between this world and the Hereafter, nor did I intend to separate the Imām and the ruler such that the Imām would be responsible for the affairs of the Hereafter while the ruler would be responsible for the affairs of this world. If I had said that, your question would have been warranted.

What I want to say is that the Shīʿa propose a different premise. If this premise is proven, the issue of government is automatically proven as well. We believe in a position that succeeds the position of prophethood. If the person who fills this position is present, there is no point in discussing the rulership of anyone else.

Just as there is no point in discussing the government of anyone else in the presence of the Prophet ﷺ, the same thing applies to the Imām ﵇ in the Shīʿa's view.

In the meaning it has today, the issue of government depends on the absence or occultation of an Imām ﵇ in this world, as is the case during our time. In the presence of the Imām ﵇ as the Shīʿa understand his role, the obligation concerning rulership and government is obvious. Both religiously and rationally, it makes more sense for the infallible Imām ﵇ to assume rulership above all others.

Question: Do Ahl al-Sunnah accept *ḥadīth* al-Ghadīr as a singular non-recurrent report or do they only believe in the narration that you mentioned where the Prophet said, "Salute ʿAlī as the Commander of the Believers"?

Answer: Even the Sunnis may not be able to deny the recurrence of this part of *ḥadīth* al-Ghadīr: "Whoever accepts me as his master, ʿAlī is his master" although Mullā al-Qūshjī does not believe in the recurrence of this part either.

The transmitters of this part of the *ḥadīth* reached such a number that Ahl al-Sunnah cannot deny its recurrence.[67] A large number of transmitters even transmitted the first part of the *ḥadīth*: "Don't I have a greater authority over you than you have over your own selves?" For this reason, the Shīʿa consider this part recurrent as well.

[67] The great number of transmitters goes back to the fact that the Prophet's ﵇ words weren't written down at that time; people sufficed themselves with oral transmission. In such circumstances, it's natural for the sentence "whoever accepts me as his master, ʿAlī is his master" to make such a strong impression on people.

As for the *ḥadīth*: "Salute ʿAlī as the Commander of the Believers," the Sunnis do not even believe in its recurrence; they consider it a singular report. Maybe we Shīʿa cannot prove its recurrence either; I'm not sure at the moment.

The recurrence of this part is not necessary in any case. The recurrence of the most important *ḥadīth* is obvious for the Shīʿa. It is the one when the Prophet asked ﷺ, "Don't I have a greater authority over you than you have over your own selves?" and they said, "Indeed." Afterward, the Prophet ﷺ said, "Whoever accepts me as his master, ʿAlī is his master. O Allah, be a guardian for whoever accepts him as master and be an enemy for his enemy."[68]

Another problem is that there is no consensus among Sunni scholars on such matters such that they all agree that a report is recurrent or singular. Some say that it is a singular report, and others say that it is recurrent.

Even the Sunnis who do agree that *ḥadīth* al-Ghadīr is recurrent do not understand it in the same way the Shīʿa do. They interpret the word *mawlā* to simply imply love. In this case, the meaning of the Prophet's ﷺ *ḥadīth* would be: "Whoever accepts me as master and loves me should love ʿAlī too."

The Shīʿa respond to this shaky logic by asking, "Did the Prophet gather the people at Ghadīr Khumm in that blazing noon heat simply to tell them that? What's the reason for this specificity? Why limit loving him and accepting his mastery to loving ʿAlī? Why did he ask, 'Don't I have a greater authority over you than you have over your own selves?'" Besides, the word *mawla* never occurred anywhere to imply love.

---

[68] *Safīnat al-biḥār*, 2/306.

Question: Was the verse: "Today I have perfected your religion for you, and I have completed My blessing upon you, and I have approved Islam as your religion"[69] revealed after the incident at Ghadīr Khumm?

Answer: No, it was revealed at Ghadīr Khumm.

---

[69] Sūrat al-Mā'ida, verse 3.

The Imamate and the Despair of the Faithless

In our previous session, we said that Shīʿa and Sunni thought about the Imamate fundamentally differs, and that this difference between the two is reconcilable. It's not that we both believe in the Imamate but differ about its conditions. The reason is that the Imamate that the Shīʿa believe in is different from the Imamate that the Sunnis believe in.

We also explained that the issue of the Imamate cannot be approached by asking whether the Imamate is determined by appointment or by consultation. In other words, we must not ask whether the Prophet ﷺ should designate the Imām ؑ or the *ummah* should elect him. The Shīʿa say that the Imamate should be by appointment whereas the Sunnis say it should be by consultation. The disagreement revolves around two things and not one thing: one side adheres to divine appointment and the other to consultation.

In other words, the Sunnis reject the Imamate as the Shīʿa understand it. It's not that they disagree with the Shīʿa about its conditions.

The issue is exactly like the disagreement between the believers in prophethood and those who deny it. The Shīʿa elevate the Imamate to such a status such that anyone who believes in it must necessarily accept that Allah ﷻ is the one who appoints the Imām ؑ, as He does with the issue of prophethood. Just as it's not said that the people come together and elect their prophet, the same applies to the Imamate for the Shīʿa; the people cannot come together and elect the Imām ؑ.

In our previous session, we discussed the degrees and conditions of the Imamate according to the Shīʿa. We concluded that the Shīʿa follow a top-down approach. If we don't want to keep the Shīʿa's doctrine about the Imamate in the realm of theory, we need to investigate whether the noble Prophet ﷺ actually appointed someone as Imām at that lofty level of the concept. We also have to see whether the Qurʾān mentioned this or not.

At first, I wanted to discuss the issue in the same order Khoja Naṣīr al-Dīn al-Ṭūsī used in his *al-Tajrīd*. However, I thought it best, as we approach the Day of al-Ghadīr, to begin with explaining the verses related to the occasion.

Today the Faithless Have Despaired of Your Religion[70]

This verse is at the beginning of Sūrat al-Māʾida, in which Allah ﷻ says, "Today [*al-yawm*] the faithless have despaired of your religion. So do not fear them, but fear Me. Today [*al-yawm*] I have perfected your religion for you, and I have completed My blessing upon you, and I have approved Islam as your religion."[71] The verse is made up of two segments that both begin with the word "today." They are two segments of one verse; not two verses, and not two segments from different verses. Both segments are related to one idea and one purpose.

I will use proofs to explain the meaning of the verse after a small discussion of the word *yawm*. The specific definite article (*al al-*

[70] [English translator's note]: Sūrat al-Māʾida, verse 3.

[71] Sūrat al-Māʾida, verse 3.

ʿ*ahdiyya)* has modified the word *yawm*; it can mean both this day and that day.

In the meaning of "that day," the word would be preceded by the mention of a specific day that the word day comes to refer to. The second meaning, as when we say, "This person came in *al-yawm*," refers to today and not that day.

The verse: "Today the faithless have despaired of your religion. So do not fear them"[72] refers to the faithless' despair. The question that arises is this: "What is the meaning of this despair?" The meaning is that they have despaired of triumphing over you and vanquishing your religion. Because they have despaired, they put a stop to their past method of confrontation, so they no longer fear them.

The wonderful thing is that this is followed by "but fear Me."[73] Since the topic is religion, the meaning is that harm will no longer come to this religion at the hands of those people. If it does suffer harm, it would necessarily be from Allah ﷻ. But what does that mean? I will answer this question later.

The remainder of the verse is: "Today I have perfected your religion for you, and I have completed My blessing upon you."[74] The verse mentions two words that are close in meaning: *al-ikāml* (perfecting) and al-*itmām* (completing).

---

[72] Sūrat al-Māʾida, verse 3.

[73] Sūrat al-Māʾida, verse 3.

[74] Sūrat al-Māʾida, verse 3.

The Difference Between Perfection and Completion

The difference between the two words is that completion is mentioned when a part is the last in a series of parts such that the thing would be deficient if not all its parts were arranged in order. If all its parts came together, including the last part, we can say that that thing is complete.

Let's take a building as an example. We don't say it's complete if its foundations were laid and its roofs and ceilings were raised. We say it's complete if it meets all the necessary conditions that make it ready for use. When it's ready for residence, it may be said to be complete.[75]

Perfection is different. The thing would not be missing a part. It might not be deficient and in need of a part to complete it, but it would still be imperfect.

An example is the fetus in its mother's womb: it reaches completion, meaning that its parts and body become complete, and it is born as a complete baby. However, it would not be a perfect person because it does not have the maturity that a person should have.

Maturity is different from having complete parts.

---

[75] [Arabic translator's note]: *al-ikmāl* is when a thing reaches its limits in terms of amount or number by sense or meaning. *Al-takmīl* is what occurs to a complete thing and perfects it; perfection is an addition to completion that is contrasted by deficiency. *Al-Kamāl* is contrasted with the deficiency in characteristics after the thing itself is completed. See *al-Kulliyāt*, Abū al-Baqāʾ Ayyūb b. Mūsā al-Ḥusaynī al-Kūfī (d. 1014), (Muʾassasat al-Risāla, 2nd edn. 1413 AH) 164, 296.

The difference between the complete and the perfect is actually a difference between quantity and quality.[76]

The Qurʾān says, "Today I have perfected your religion for you"[77] and "I have completed My blessing upon you."[78] It finally adds: "and I have approved Islam as your religion."[79] This last verse means that Islam today finally became the Islam that Allah ﷻ wants. Clearly, the meaning isn't that this Islam is the same Islam as before but Allah ﷻ changed His mind.

The meaning is that after Islam was completed and reached perfection, it became now the divine religion that Allah ﷻ approves of. The religion that Allah ﷻ wants is this complete, perfect Islam.

[76] [Arabic translator's note]: Abū al-Hilāl al-ʿAskarī has said, "Completion removes essential deficiencies and perfection removes deficiencies in attributes after the essence is completed." It is said that this is why *ʿashara kāmila* in Sūrat al-Baqara (verse 96) is more eloquent than *ʿashara tāmma.* This is because a *tāmm* number may have deficient attributes. It is also said that completion gives the impression of prior deficiency whereas perfection does not. Abū al-Hilāl al-ʿAskarī said, "Perfection is the coming together of the described thing's parts whereas completion refers to the part that completes the described thing. This is why it is said that the rhyme (*qāfiya*) completes the verse but does not perfect it. They say that a verse requires its own perfection or its coming together in succession." See *Furūq al-lughāt fil-tamyīz bayn al-kalimāt,* Nūr al-Dīn b. Niʿmat Allāh al-Jazāʾirī, 44, n. 26, 3rd edn., Tehran 1415 AH).

[77] Sūrat al-Māʾida, verse 3.

[78] Sūrat al-Māʾida, verse 3.

[79] Sūrat al-Māʾida, verse 3.

This is the meaning of the verse.[80]

As for the word "today," everything about it revolves around this question: "What day is meant here?" What day was so important that the Qur'ān said that it was the day when religion was perfected and divine blessing was completed? This day must have been very important; an extraordinary incident must have happened on it.

It is not an incident that concerns only the Shīʿa or only the Sunnis.

An amazing thing about these verses is that nothing before or after them signifies that day. Nothing about that day can be understood from the textual evidence itself.

The verse could have mentioned an important issue or incident and said, "Today..." to comment on the occasion. However, this did not happen. The verse was actually preceded by the stipulation of very simple rulings related to lawful and unlawful animal flesh. While the verse mentions that carrion, blood, and pork are prohibited, the text suddenly surprises us with Allah's ﷻ saying, "Today the faithless have despaired of your religion. So do not fear them, but

[80] [Arabic translator's note]: al-ʿAllāma al-Ṭabāṭabāʾī says about this verse, "Perfecting and completing are close in meaning. Al-Rāghib al-Iṣfahānī said, 'The perfection of a thing is the achievement of its purpose, whereas its completion means reaching a point where it does not need anything external to it. A deficient thing needs something external to it.' You can also determine the meaning of the two words in a different way. The consequences of things are of two kinds. Some consequences follow when all the parts of a thing are there, if it has parts, such as if some of its parts or conditions were missing, the thing itself would be invalid. An example is fasting. The fast is invalid if it is broken during the day. Such an example entails completion: "Then complete the fast until nightfall" (Sūrat al-Baqara, verse 187). The second kind of consequences follow without all the parts of the thing; the consequence of the whole is the same as the consequence of the parts. Allah ﷻ says, "As for someone who cannot afford [the offering], let him fast three days during the hajj and seven when you return; that is [a period of] ten complete [days]' (Sūrat al-Baqara, verse 196). The consequences of the numbers apply to the part and the whole. In Allah's ﷻ saying, "Today I have perfected your religion for you, and I have completed My blessing upon you," religion means the total of knowledge and legislated rulings. This total has had something added to it today. The blessing, regardless of what it is, is one moral thing that was deficient and did not have a consequence but was completed and caused its consequence." *Al-Mizān*, 5/179-80.

fear Me. Today I have perfected your religion for you, and I have completed My blessing upon you, and I have approved Islam as your religion."[81] After this digression, the text returns to its original context, mentioning the ruling on compulsion: "But should anyone be compelled by hunger, without inclining to sin, then Allah ﷻ is indeed all-forgiving, all-merciful."[82]

The text was arranged in a way that if we removed this middle part that we are discussing, the first and third parts would flow without the slightest disruption in context. This also happens in two or three other places in the Qur'ān. In contrast, this middle section is not related to the other two parts and it expresses a complete, independent idea.[83]

Which Day?

Shīʿa and Sunni exegetes made efforts to determine the day mentioned in the verse. This may be done using two methods. The first method is to determine the meaning and understand it from the evidence within the verse. In other words, this method requires understanding the context to see which day may be meant. The second method requires going back to history and *ḥadīths* to understand the reason the verse was revealed.

---

[81] Sūrat al-Mā'ida, verse 3.

[82] Sūrat al-Mā'ida, verse 3.

[83] [Arabic translator's note]: The author means that the beginning of the verse: "You are prohibited carrion and blood" (Sūrat al-Mā'ida, verse 3) is related to its ending. The two are a complete whole and a singular textual unit that does not depend on the middle part where Allah ﷻ says, "Today the faithless have despaired of your religion." If we omitted this part, the context would not be disrupted. There are other verses that directly mention prohibited foods, such as in Sūrat al-An'ām, Sūrat al-Naḥl, and Sūrat al-Baqara. For example, in Sūrat al-Baqara we find: "He has forbidden you only carrion, blood, the flesh of the swine, and that which has been offered to other than Allah. But should someone be compelled, without being rebellious or aggressive, there shall be no sin upon him. Indeed Allah is all-forgiving, all-merciful." (Sūrat al-Baqara, verse 173). The Same thing occurs in Sūrat al-An'ām and Sūrat al-Naḥl.

The group that chose the first method say that they have nothing to do with the time and occasion of the verse's revelation as mentioned in history, the *sunnah*, and *ḥadīth.* These people only look at the content of the verse. Their conclusion was that the verse concerns the time of the Prophet's ﷺ mission. The word "today" then refers to a day in the past, i.e. the day the Prophet ﷺ received his mission.

These verses are at the beginning of Sūrat al-Māʾida. This is the fifth *sūra* in the Qurʾān, which opened with the words: "O you who have faith! Keep your agreements."[84] All exegetes agree that Sūrat al-Māʾida was the last *sūra* to be revealed to the Prophet ﷺ. This means it's a Medinan *sūra.* This *sūra* was revealed even after Sūrat al-Fatḥ.

One or two verses were revealed after Sūrat al-Māʾida and included in other *sūras,* but no other complete *sūra* was revealed after it. For this reason, its verses are of the last verses that were revealed to the Prophet ﷺ.

Different Theories

There are a number of theories on the meaning of "today" in the verse. I will mention three of them.

The Day of the Prophet's ﷺ Mission

I already mentioned that some people say that "today" refers to that day and not today. What's the proof for this?

---

[84] Sūrat al-Māʾida, verse 1.

They say that the "today" when Allah ﷻ approved of Islam has to be the day the Prophet ﷺ received his mission. The proof is the verse: "I have approved Islam as your religion."[85]

This could've been true if the verse wasn't preceded by the verses that spoke of perfecting Allah's ﷻ religion and completing his blessing. This is because the beginning of the prophetic mission was the actual beginning of this blessing.

The verse "I have approved Islam as your religion"[86] means that the Islam that has been perfected and completed in blessing is the approved Islam.

The Conquest of Mecca

Another opinion proposed without proof is that the word "today" refers to the day Mecca was conquered. The proponents of this opinion mentioned that this day is one of the great days in the history of Islam, and they are right. On that day, Allah ﷻ said, "Indeed We have inaugurated for you a clear victory that Allah may forgive you what is past of your sin and what is to come."[87]

Mecca had an important spiritual dimension in the Arabian Peninsula. After the Year of the Elephant and the marvelous defeat of the Men of the Elephant,[88] all the peninsula's tribes deeply believed in the Kaʿba as a great place of worship.

---

[85] Sūrat al-Māʾida, verse 3.

[86] Sūrat al-Māʾida, verse 3.

[87] Sūrat al-Fatḥ, verses 1 and 2.

[88] [English translator's note]: See Sūrat al-Fīl, verse 1.

The arrogance of Quraysh lies in this point. They used the Kaʿba's importance for their own advantage, speaking of their own position and importance and the respect they deserve.

The story of the Men of the Elephant ended with that divine tribulation that struck their army and annihilated them. The tribe of Quraysh became arrogant after this incident and used the Kaʿba to make the other tribes subordinate to it.

The market of Mecca prospered, and Quraysh began ordering people left and right. People obeyed because of the psychological and religious dimension that the Kaʿba kindled in them.

Since that time, people felt that the Kaʿba can never be dominated by anyone.

It happened that the Prophet ﷺ conquered Mecca without bloodshed, trouble, or even the slightest harm. Perhaps the Prophet ﷺ took this psychological and religious feeling into account when he conquered Mecca without bloodshed.

If a hundred or more Muslims had died during any other battle, it would've passed without comment. However, if they suffered the slightest harm during the conquest of Mecca, it would've been said, "Muḥammad and his companions met the same fate of the Men of the Elephant."

In the conquest of Mecca, the Prophet ﷺ followed an approach that didn't cause the spilling of one drop of blood from either side. The only exception to this is Khālid b. al-Walīd and his grudgeful nature. When he reached some polytheists at the outskirts of Mecca, he killed some of them after they resisted him. When the Prophet ﷺ heard about it, he dissociated himself from Khālid's deed, saying, "O Allah, I dissociate myself before You from what Khālid b. al-Walīd has done."[89]

The conquest of Mecca had a deep psychological impact on the Arabian tribes. They had the chance to consider the issue from a different perspective: here was Muḥammad who came and conquered Mecca without being harmed at all.

After this incident, the Peninsula embraced Islam, and its people came to the Prophet ﷺ and chose Islam voluntarily.

There is a verse where Allah ﷻ says, "Not equal [to others] are those of you who spent and fought before the victory than those who have spent and fought afterwards."[90]

This is because the Muslims were few before the conquest of Mecca, and their acts came out of pure faith. After the conquest, people chose Islam as a matter of course.

Faith after the conquest of Mecca is not like faith before it.

There is no doubt that the conquest of Mecca was a great victory for Islam. That's unquestionable.

---

[89] [Arabic translator's note]: This incident happened when Khālid b. al-Walīd went out to Banū Judhayma to call them to Islam while the Prophet ﷺ was still in Mecca. This means that the incident did not take place in Mecca. When Khālid dismounted, he was met with raised weapons. During pre-Islamic times, Banū Judhayma had killed al-Fākih b. al-Mughīra, Khālid's paternal uncle. Eventually, the two tribes decided to put their differences aside. Khālid, however, had those who met him tied up, and he killed some of them. Al-Ṭabarī and Ibn Hishām state that an argument broke out between Khālid and ʿAbd al-Raḥmān b. ʿAwf who was with Khālid at the time. ʿAbd al-Raḥmān accused Khālid of killing the members of Banū Judhayma to avenge his uncle. When the Prophet ﷺ heard, he raised his hands up to the sky in supplication and said, "O Allah, I dissociate myself before You from what Khālid b. al-Walīd has done." A narration states that he said it three times. The Prophet ﷺ sent ʿAlī ؑ to pay the blood money and recompense their financial losses. See Sīra, Ibn Hishām, 4/70ff.

[90] Sūrat al-Ḥadīd, verse 10.

Now, we go back to the possibility that the verse concerns the conquest of Mecca. We previously mentioned that there is no historical or linguistic proof of this opinion.

Aside from lacking historical support, the content of the verse itself does not support this view. The meaning of "Today I have perfected your religion for you, and I have completed My blessing upon you" [91]is that Allah ﷻ did not leave anything without clarifying it. However, we know that many of the rulings and teachings of Islam were revealed after the conquest of Mecca. This contradicts the part of the verse that says, "I have completed My blessing upon you."[92] When someone says, "I completed the construction of this building," it surely doesn't mean that he left it half-finished.

Many verses were revealed after the conquest of Mecca, including Sūrat al-Māʾida; it's a long *sūra* with many rulings and teachings. How can it be said that this part of the *sūra* is related to the conquest of Mecca that happened in the eighth year of the Hijra although the *sūra* itself was revealed in the tenth year of the Hijra?

If we assume that this verse alone was revealed during the conquest of Mecca, it still wouldn't relate to the completion of Allah's ﷻ blessing.

Another objection to this assumption is related to this part of the verse: "Today the faithless have despaired of your religion."[93] Was this the situation during the conquest of Mecca? It's true that the conquest had a great impact, but did the faithless entirely despair of vanquishing Islam then? Of course not.

---

[91] Sūrat al-Māʾida, verse 3.

[92] Sūrat al-Māʾida, verse 3.

[93] Sūrat al-Māʾida, verse 3.

The Promulgation of Sūrat Barāʾa

Another important day that the verse may be referring to is the day Imām ʿAlī ☙ recited Sūrat Barāʾa at Minā during year nine of the Hijra. The conquest of Mecca was a military conquest that had an amazing impact, which established the military and even the spiritual power of Islam. Despite that, the Prophet ☙ was still living alongside the polytheists based on a reconciliation agreement (ṣulḥ). According to the agreement, the polytheists had the right to circumambulate (ṭawāf) the Kaʿba, stay in Mecca, and participate in the pilgrimage.

One year the pilgrimage was common between the Muslims and the polytheists; the Muslims performed their rites based on the teachings of Islam, and the polytheists performed their own rites. In the ninth year of the Hijra, Sūrat Barāʾa [al-Tawba] was revealed, and the Prophet ☙ chose Imām ʿAlī ☙ to recite it for all to hear. According to this sūra, the polytheists were no longer allowed to participate in the pilgrimage rites, and the pilgrimage turned into a rite for the Muslims alone.

The story is well-known. The Prophet ☙ sent Abū Bakr as the leader of the pilgrims, and the latter was still on the way when Sūrat Barāʾa was revealed. Exegetes disagree about whether Abū Bakr went to promulgate Sūrat Barāʾa or whether he was only the leader of the pilgrims.

Both the Shīʿa and the Sunnis agree on the following fact and count it as a merit for Imām ʿAlī ☙. The Prophet ☙ sent Imām ʿAlī ☙ on his own she-camel, al-ʿAḍbāʾ, after he received revelation telling him, "Only you or a man of you can communicate this sūra." Because of this, Imām ʿAlī ☙ caught up with Abū Bakr on the way.

It's mentioned that when the Prophet ﷺ sent Imām ʿAlī ؑ, Abū Bakr was inside his tent [or according to another narration on the way] when he heard the grunting of the Prophet's she-camel. He went out in a fright thinking it was the Prophet ﷺ. When he saw that it was Imām ʿAlī ؑ, he knew that something important had happened. Imām ʿAlī ؑ told Abū Bakr that the Prophet ﷺ was told that only a man of his is allowed to promulgate this *sūra.* Abū Bakr went back to Medina, worried that revelation concerning him came down and angered the Prophet ﷺ. He asked the Prophet ﷺ, "O Prophet of Allah, did you receive a revelation about me?" The Prophet ﷺ said, "No, but I was commanded to promulgate this *sūra* myself or send a man of me."[94]

This is the point of disagreement. The Sunnis relate that Imām ʿAlī ؑ recited the verse and Abū Bakr continued on his trip, and the mission that the Prophet ﷺ assigned to Abū Bakr remained the same except for the promulgation of the *sūra* [in other words, he was still the leader of the pilgrims]. However, the Shīʿa and many Sunnis say that Abū Bakr went back to Medina. According to al-ʿAllāma al-Ṭabāṭabāʾī, when Abū Bakr saw the Prophet ﷺ, he

---

[94] [Arabic translator's note]: The text of the lectures is confused since the Shaykh was giving an oral lecture, translating, and explaining at the same time. The historical text is mixed up with the translation and explanation at times, which leads to confusion. I tried my best to preserve the historical nature of the incident by arranging the text accordingly. Innumerable sources related this incident. In *Tafsīr al-Burhān,* Ibn Shahrāshūb says that this *ḥadīth* is mentioned by al-Ṭabrisī, al-Balādhurī, al-Tirmidhī, al-Wāqidī, al-Shaʿbī, al-Suddī, al-Thaʿlabī, al-Wāḥidī, al-Qurṭubī, al-Qushayrī, al-Samʿānī, Aḥmad b. Ḥanbal, Ibn Baṭṭa, Muḥammad b. Isḥāq, Abū Yaʿlā al-Mawṣillī, al-Aʿmash, and Simāk b. Ḥarb in their books. They narrated from ʿUrwa b. al-Zubayr, Abū Hurayra, Anas, Abū Rāfiʿ, Zayd b. Nafiʿ, Ibn ʿUmar, and Ibn ʿAbbās. Ibn ʿAbbās said, "When nine verses from Sūrat Barāʾa were revealed, the Prophet sent Abū Bakr to Mecca to promulgate it. However, Jibrāʾīl came down and said, 'Only you or a man of you can promulgate this *sūra.*' The Prophet told ʿAlī, 'Ride my she-camel, al-ʿAḍbāʾ, catch up with Abū Bakr, and take Barāʾa from him.' When Abū Bakr came back to the Prophet, he was distressed and said, 'O Prophet of Allah, you sent me on a mission about which everyone envied me, but when I set out on my way you turned me back.' The Prophet said, 'Jibrāʾīl came down to me and said that Allah ﷻ says, 'Only you or a man of you can promulgate this *sūra,* and ʿAlī is of me. Only ʿAlī can promulgate on my behalf.' See *al-Sīra,* Ibn Hishām, 4/190; *Tārīkh al-Yaʿqūbī,* volume 2; *Tafsīr al-Qummī,* ʿAlī b. Ibrāhīm, 281ff; *Faḍāʾil al-khamsa,* Hāshim Maʿrūf al-Ḥasanī, 677.

asked, "O Prophet of Allah, did you receive a revelation about me?" The Prophet ﷺ said, "No."[95]

This means that the promulgation of Sūrat Barā'a was an exceptional day in the life of the Muslims. On that day, it was announced that the Sacred Precinct (al-Ḥaram) belongs to the Muslims alone and that the polytheists are no longer allowed to participate in the pilgrimage.

This declaration made the polytheists understand that they cannot persist in their polytheism. Islam coexists with other religions like Judaism, Christianity, and Zoroastrianism, but it cannot withstand polytheism and coexist with it.

Given this day's importance, some said that it may be the day referred to in Sūrat al-Mā'ida. The response to this proposition is that it does not conform to the meaning of "I have completed My blessing upon you"[96] because many rulings were revealed after this day. In contrast, the day referred to in the verse must be toward the end of the Prophet's ﷺ life such that no other rulings were revealed. [97]

---

[95] [Arabic translator's note]: *al-Mīzān*, volume 9, 161ff. I would like to point out the importance of al-ʿAllāma al-Ṭabāṭabā'ī's ideas and the richness of his textual discussion of the incident.

[96] Sūrat al-Mā'ida, verse 3.

[97] Some parts of our discussion have appeared in the book *Khilāfat va-vilāyat* [in Persian] by Muḥammad Taqī Sharīʿatī. It was published by Husayniyya-i Irshād recently. Muḥammad Taqī Sharīʿatī gave his conclusions in lecture form at Ḥusayniyya-i Irshād four years ago based on Sūrat al-Mā'ida. What he said might've required more elaboration. Perhaps what I'm saying will help clarify his words a little, and perhaps if you read the book yourselves, it will help you understand what I'm saying. What I mean is that both my lectures and his clarify each other.

The Opinion of the Shīʿa

The Shīʿa say that the content of the verse and the historical proofs support their opinion. Since both textual and historical proof support this opinion, we should discuss it at two levels: 1- the textual and 2- the historical.

The Historical Dimension

If we want to begin with the second part of the discussion, we are dealing with a very detailed historical incident. The majority of the books that discussed this topic mostly relied on the historical dimension and the dimension of *ḥadīth*, which proved that the verse was revealed at Ghadīr Khumm.[98]

Kitāb al-Ghadīr [eleven volumes] was dedicated to proving this proposition. Historians and *ḥadīth* compilers strove to prove the reality of the incident. If we go back to *Tārīkh al-Yaʿqūbī*,[99] which is one of the oldest historical books in Islam, and which is esteemed by both the Sunnis and the Shīʿa, we will find that it mentions the incident at Ghadīr Khumm.

The narration mentions that when the Prophet ﷺ went back from Mecca to Medina after the farewell pilgrimage,[100] he reached a spot

---

[98] [Arabic translator's note]: *Tārīkh al-Yaʿqūbī* (Beirut, Dār Ṣādir, 2/112.

[99] *Tārīkh al-Yaʿqūbī* is a very well-written book. It was written at the beginning of the third Hijri century after the reign of al-Maʾmūn and around the reign of al-Mutawakkil. It is more than just a book of *ḥadīth* and history in its value.

[100] The farewell pilgrimage took place in the last year of the Prophet's ﷺ life, two months before he passed away to be more precise. The Prophet ﷺ arrived at Ghadīr Khumm on the 18th of Dhū al-Ḥijja, i.e. two months and ten days before his passing if he passed on the 28th of Ṣafar according to the calculations of the Shīʿa. If he passed away on the twelfth of Rabīʿ al-Awwal according to the calculations of the Sunnis, we would have arrived at Ghadīr Khumm two months and twenty days from his death.

near al-Juḥfa[101] called Ghadīr Khumm. He stopped the caravan and gathered the Muslims to preach to them. This was when the verse was revealed. The Prophet ﷺ ordered setting up a pulpit, so a pulpit was made for him out of camel saddles. The Prophet ﷺ mounted the saddle and spoke to the people. He asked, "Don't I have a greater authority over you than you have over your own selves?" They said, "Indeed." The Prophet ﷺ then said, "Whoever accepts me as his master, ʿAlī is his master."

After the Prophet ﷺ fulfilled his duty, the verse "Today the faithless have despaired of your religion. So do not fear them, but fear Me. Today I have perfected your religion for you, and I have completed My blessing upon you" was revealed.

If we want to discuss the issue from the historical perspective, we should go over the books of the Shīʿa and the Sunnis one by one, and particularly the books of the Sunnis that mentioned and transmitted the incident.

These matters have been discussed in books like *al-Ghadīr* [and *al-ʿAbaqāt*]. There's also a book that's been published a few years ago by Muʾassasat Nashr al-Ḥaqāʾiq that basically summarizes the issue of al-Ghadīr. Perhaps the esteemed audience members would benefit from reading it.

From the historical perspective, the Shīʿa go back to history to find out what is meant by the word "today" in the verse "Today I have

[101] Al-Juḥfa is the pilgrimage post (*mīqāt*) of Ahl al-Shām. The pilgrims coming from the road of al-Shām northwest to Mecca arrive at al-Juḥfa after crossing some distance. Al-Juḥfa is a post that the Prophet ﷺ designated for people coming on that road, and Ghadīr Khumm is close to it. It is like a crossroads because all the Muslims went back home from it; the people of Medina back to Medina and all the others to their own regions. [Arabic translator's note: Afterward, the author mentions Jedda and discusses whether it may be taken as a pilgrimage post or not. He explains that the answer depends not on legal opinions but on geography. If it was proven that Jedda is adjacent to other posts, it could be taken as a starting point toward Mecca].

perfected your religion."[102] If we do so, we will discover that the fruit of our efforts will not be not one or two or even ten narrations. There is a recurrence around the verse's revelation on the day of Ghadīr Khumm after the Prophet ﷺ appointed ʿAlī ؑ as his successor.

Proofs from the Verse Itself

Now we want to take a look at the verse and see whether it contains proofs that support the facts of history. The verse says, "Today the faithless have despaired of your religion."[103] This is similar to many other Qurʾānic verses that warned the Muslims that the polytheists were constantly scheming against them and their religion, eager for them to apostate. These warnings also included the People of the Book as well; Allah ﷻ says, "Many of the People of the Book are eager to turn you into unbelievers after your faith, out of their inner envy."[104]

In other words, Allah ﷻ warns the Muslims in the Qurʾān that the polytheists are eager to demolish their religion, but He mentions in this verse that the polytheists have despaired of defeating Islam. Their hostility toward Islam was put to an end: "So do not fear them, but fear Me."[105] If your faith later weakens or is eradicated, if anything happens to you, it is Me you have to fear. What does this mean? Does it mean that Allah ﷻ is an enemy of His own religion? No, the verse discusses a Qurʾānic concept that appears in many verses. This concept was presented as a basic principle that includes all the blessings that Allah ﷻ bestowed on His servants. Allah ﷻ

[102] Sūrat al-Māʾida, verse 3.

[103] Sūrat al-Māʾida, verse 3.

[104] Sūrat al-Baqara, verse 109

[105] Sūrat al-Māʾida, verse 3.

says, "Indeed Allah does not change a people's lot, unless they change what is in their souls."[106] Elsewhere, He says, "That is because Allah never changes a blessing that He has bestowed on a people unless they change what is in their own souls."[107]

The point is that Allah ﷻ never deprives people of His blessing unless they desire this themselves. This idea expresses a basic Qur᾿ānic principle.

Ambiguous and Unambiguous Verses

Since we mentioned this verse, I think I should speak of a matter that comes up often. The verses of the Qur᾿ān interpret one another: "Parts of the Qur᾿ān interpret one another." The Qur᾿ānic is a clear and clarifying book which classifies its verses into two categories: unambiguous verses (*muḥkamāt*) and ambiguous verses (*mutashābihāt*). The unambiguous verses are called the mother of the Book: "It is He who has sent down to you the Book. Parts of it are unambiguous verses, which are the mother of the Book, while others are ambiguous."[108] An ambiguous verse contains concepts that may be applied in more than one way. An unambiguous verse, in contrast, contains a concept that can only be applied in one way. The Qur᾿ān called these latter verses the mother of the Book because even ambiguous verses can be determined and applied based on them.

If a verse may be applied in more than one way, we cannot apply it except after referring back to the other verses of the Qur᾿ān. This act of reference informs us of how to apply the verse. An

[106] Sūrat al-Raʿd, verse 11.

[107] Sūrat al-Anfāl, verse 53.

[108] Sūrat al-Āl ᾿Imrān, verse 7. [English translator's note]: Translation changed slightly.

ambiguous verse is not an overly general verse or a verse with obscure words; it is a verse that may be explained in many similar ways.

For example, in the Qur'ān there are verses related to absolute divine will. These verses attribute everything without exception to divine will. Of these verses, which are ambiguous, is the following: "Say, 'O Allah, Master of all sovereignty! You give sovereignty to whomever You wish, and strip of sovereignty whomever You wish; You make mighty whomever You wish, and You abase whomever You wish; all good is in Your hand. Indeed You have power over all things."[109] There is no clearer indication that Allah ﷻ is the original master of all sovereignty and power: He bestows sovereignty and might on whoever He wills and strips them away from whoever He wills, and all good is in His ﷻ hand.

This verse is ambiguous because it can apply to different aspects. It states that everything happens according to the will of Allah ﷻ. This may have two meanings. According to the first meaning, nothing may be a condition of anything else. This mistaken meaning was concluded from the verse by some people who said, "All the conditions of might could be present, but the result of those conditions would still be an abasement instead of might." Similarly, all the conditions of abasement could be present, but the result of those conditions would be might instead of abasement!

The logic of these people is that when it comes to the happiness in this world and the Hereafter, nothing may be a condition or a cause of something else because everything happens by the will of Allah ﷻ.

---

[109] Sūrat al-Āl 'Imrān, verse 26.

According to this logic, an individual or a group of people can attain perfect happiness in this world without preliminaries or any effort, and they can attain perfect misery without cause as well. In addition, people may reach ʾIlliyūn without any cause or condition while others may fall to the bottom of Sijjīn without preliminaries.

It is unfortunate that a group of Muslims called the Ashʾarites used the verse like this and said that there is no problem in a prophet being led to Hell while Abū Jahl goes to Paradise because Allah ﷻ said that everything happens according to divine will.

This is undoubtedly an incorrect application of the verse. The verse only mentions that everything depends on divine will, but it doesn't explain how this divine will works and how it affects happiness, misery, might, and abasement.

This verse can be applied in more than one way; it's an example of an ambiguous verse. When we look at other verses in the Qurʾān, we find that they are unambiguous, or the mother of the Book that explains the ambiguous verses. For example, the verse clearly says, "That is because Allah never changes a blessing that He has bestowed on a people unless they change what is in their own souls."[110] The other, more general verse states: "Indeed Allah does not change a people's lot, unless they change what is in their souls."[111]

Each of these two verses includes elements absent from the other. The second verse tells us that Allah ﷻ does not strip away His blessings from people until they strip it away themselves first.

---

110 Sūrat al-Anfāl, verse 53.

111 Sūrat al-Raʿd, verse 11.

This is a general verse meaning that Allah ﷻ does not strip away a people's blessing or change it into punishment unless they changed first. Similarly, He does not change a people's punishment into a blessing unless they changed first. The first verse discusses blessings without mentioning punishments, but it adds the detail of "That is because Allah never changes a blessing [*lam yaku mughayyiran*]." This means that Allah ﷻ has never done this. Similarly, whenever we encounter "because Allah never (*mā kāna Allah*)" in the Qurʾān, it means that Allah's ﷻ Lordship (*rubūbiyya*) forbids this. It is against Lordship for a Lord to arbitrarily and randomly strip people's blessings away.

Saying that Allah's ﷻ Will works arbitrarily and randomly and that consequences have no conditions goes against the wisdom (*ḥikma*) of Allah ﷻ and the perfection of His essence (*dhāt*) and lordship.

This is why some verses are considered the mother of the Book.

What the [ambiguous] verses on divine will are saying is that everything happens by the will of Allah ﷻ. As for this [unambiguous] verse, it is telling us that Allah ﷻ works this way and according to this law.

When we go back to the Qurʾān, then, we find that the issue expresses itself through a basic principle that is solid and sound. This principle was repeatedly mentioned in many verses. This principle is the following: If you are grateful for My blessing, meaning if you benefit from it properly, I will keep it, but if you are ungrateful, I will strip it away.

The above explains the meaning of the verse: "Today the faithless have despaired of your religion. So do not fear them, but fear Me."

[112]It means that the faithless who do not belong to the Islamic community have despaired of uprooting your religion, and they are no longer a danger to the Islamic world. What is asked of you now is to "fear Me," meaning fear your own doings.

It is as though Allah ﷻ is saying this: O Muslims, if there is still a danger after this day, it is your ill-treatment of the blessing that is Islam. If you are ungrateful for this blessing and do not benefit from it properly, then the law of "Indeed Allah does not change a people's lot, unless they change what is in their souls"[113] will apply to you.

There is no longer any danger threatening Islam from without; the danger is within.

Audience Q & A

Question: We believe, like you kindly said, that the Imamate concerns religion and this world, which is a position specific to Imām ʿAlī ؑ based on the presented evidence. My question is why did the Imām ؑ hesitate to accept the people's pledge of allegiance when they came to him after ʿUthmān was killed? It was not the time for hesitation. Shouldn't he have accepted their pledge immediately?

Answer: This question was raised in the recently published book, *Khilāfat va-vilāyat.* The answer is apparent in the words of Imām ʿAlī ؑ himself. When they came to him to pledge allegiance, he said, "Leave me be and seek someone else. We're coming upon something that has many facets and components." That's an amazing answer; he said that there are many facets and not just one.

---

[112] Sūrat al-Māʾida, verse 3.

[113] Sūrat al-Raʿd, verse 11.

He continued by saying, "The horizon became clouded, and the way became obscured." He means that the clear path that was once set by the Prophet ﷺ became unknown and obscured, and the sky became overcast with clouds.

After that, he told them that if he ruled them, "I will rule you based on what I know." He means that he would act based on his own knowledge and not on their personal whims.

These words make it clear that Imām ʿAlī ﵇ knew very well that the situation was completely different from the days of the Prophet ﷺ. The difference between the two times was like the difference between heaven and earth. This was very clear to Imām ʿAlī ﵇. This was historically proved: things changed to an amazing degree and ended in havoc.

The Imām ﵇ said these words to make the people accountable (*itmām al-ḥujja*). This is because a pledge of allegiance is a pledge to obey and follow. The caliphate of Imām ʿAlī ﵇ would not be invalid without a pledge of allegiance; a pledge of allegiance simply means pledging to obey and follow the Imām ﵇.

There is an incident that both the Sunnis and the Shīʿa narrate . When ʿUmar chose the members of the consultation (*shūrā*), Imām ʿAlī ﵇ was one of them. Three members of the consultation sided with the other three: al-Zubayr sided with ʿAlī ﵇, Ṭalḥa sided with ʿUthmān, and Saʿd b. Abī al-Waqqāṣ sided with ʿAbd al-Raḥmān b. ʿAwf. When the candidates were down to three, ʿAbd al-Raḥmān declared that he did not want the position. This left ʿAlī and ʿUthmān. ʿAbd al-Raḥmān b. ʿAwf had the deciding vote; whoever he chose became the caliph.

ʿAbd al-Raḥmān b. ʿAwf came to Imām ʿAlī ﷺ at first, and he told him that he was ready to pledge allegiance to him on the condition that he would abide by the Book of Allah, the *sunnah* of the Prophet ﷺ, and the way of the two Shaykhs [Abū Bakr and ʿUmar]. Imām ʿAlī ﷺ said he was ready to accept the caliphate and abide by the Book of Allah and the *sunnah* of the Prophet ﷺ alone, without the way of the two Shaykhs.

ʿAbd al-Raḥmān then went to ʿUthmān and made the same offer to him. ʿUthmān agreed to the condition of abiding by the Book of Allah, the *sunnah* of the Prophet ﷺ, and the way of the two Shaykhs. The funny thing is that ʿUthmān did not keep his word about abiding by the way of the two Shaykhs, as Muḥammad Taqī Sharīʿatī mentions in *Khilāfat va-vilāyat.*

The way of the Imām ʿAlī ﷺ was the way of the Prophet ﷺ. If we compare the way of Imām ʿAlī ﷺ to the way of the two Shaykhs, the way of Imām ʿAlī ﷺ was similar to the way of the two Shaykhs. This is because Abū Bakr and ʿUmar largely abided by the way of the Prophet ﷺ. Despite this, Imām ʿAlī ﷺ refused to abide by their way because agreeing to do so would mean approving the deviations that appeared during their reigns and losing the ability to confront these deviations in the future.

For example, the practice of favoritism began during ʿUmar's reign when he began discriminating between the Emigrants and the Helpers on the one hand, and between Emigrants and the Helpers and other people on the other hand. Imām ʿAlī ﷺ was steadfastly against this. Abiding by the way of the two Shaykhs would have meant reinforcing this discrimination and division. He ﷺ did not want to do that because Imām ʿAlī ﷺ did not want to deceive and lie, pretending to accept the condition today and refusing it tomorrow; he refused the condition from the start. Imām ʿAlī ﷺ

refused to follow the way of his predecessors despite the small number of deviations. This is why it was natural for him to tell the *ummah* that if he governed, he would rule based on his knowledge and not their whims, especially because after ʿUthmān the situation changed dramatically. As Imām ʿAlī ﷷ said, the horizon became clouded and many new facets and components emerged, and the people wanted Imām ʿAlī ﷷ to rule them as they liked.

This means that Imām ʿAlī ﷷ said what he said not because he was refusing to govern but because he wanted to make people accountable.

Question: The Qurʾān itself greatly stresses the issue of unity. When we consider the importance of the Imamate in general and the Imamate of Imām ʿAlī ﷷ in particular, the following question arises. Why didn't the Qurʾān explicitly address this issue, and why didn't the Prophet ﷺ speak of it on various occasions?

Answer: This is a two-part question: 1- Why didn't the Qurʾān explicitly mention this issue? Did the noble Prophet speak of it on various occasions or not? Another question is whether the Qurʾān mentioned the issue [without explicitly naming names] in various verses.

Concerning the second part of your question, I want to say that the issue is a historical one. Many Sunnis have said that the Prophet ﷺ had spoken of the issue on various occasions, and that his declaration was not limited to Ghadīr Khumm. They wrote about this in books on the Imamate. The Prophet ﷺ said, "Your position from me is like Hārūn's position from Mūsā except that there is no prophet after me" in Tabūk.

The Prophet ﷺ also explained the position of ʿAlī ؑ in Khaybar when he said, "Tomorrow I will give the banner to a man who loves Allah and His Prophet and whom Allah and His Prophet love." The Prophet ﷺ even confirmed this at the beginning of his mission when he spoke to his tribe and asked, "Which one among you will assist me in this and in return be my brother, legatee, and successor among you?" That man was none other than ʿAlī ؑ.

The Qurʾān followed the same method; it did not mention the topic just once or twice. The question that remains is why didn't the noble Qurʾān explicitly name names?

Interestingly, this issue also was raised in *Khilāfat va-vilāyat.* Our doctrine states that the Qurʾān transcends distortion: no additions or deletions have been made to it. The name of Imām ʿAlī ؑ was never explicitly mentioned in it.

This question has been answered in two ways. The first way was mentioned in *Khilāfat va-vilāyat,* where it was explained well. Its summary is that the Qurʾān follows a certain methodology when explaining topics. It always explains the principle without individual and personal specifications. This itself is a merit of the Qurʾān. When Allah ﷻ says, "Today the faithless have despaired of your religion,"[114] The despair of the faithless goes back to the nature of their wager. They used to say, "As long as this Prophet ﷺ is around, nothing can be done, but as soon as he dies this religion will be over." This was the last hope of the Prophet's ؑ opponents, but they despaired when they saw the noble Prophet ﷺ addressing this issue and arranging for the persistence of the *ummah.* This happened when he ؑ told the *ummah* its obligation after him.

114 Sūrat al-Māʾida, verse 3.

The second way of answering refers to the Prophet's fear for the future of the *ummah* in his last days. Ahl al-Sunnah mentioned this too. This fear of the Prophet ﷺ coincided with the fear in the Qur'ān in the verse: "fear Me."[115] The Prophet ﷺ was worried about the future of the *ummah,* anxious about the threats within. Ahl al-Sunnah themselves narrate that the Prophet ﷺ went out on one of his final nights to al-Baqī'. Abū Muwayhiba followed him. The Prophet ﷺ stood and began asking forgiveness for the people buried in al-Baqī', and one of the things he said was, "How fortunate you are to be here; tribulations like pieces of the dark night are coming."[116]

This text indicates that the Prophet ﷺ was announcing the beginning of tribulations after him. Undoubtedly, the matter of the caliphate itself is one of the tribulations. We can make the following conclusions about no names being explicitly mentioned. First of all, the noble Qur'ān explains principles. Secondly, the noble Prophet ﷺ—or Allah ﷻ—did not want to be explicit considering the whims that could affect the matter. The proof of this is what happened; the people expressed all sorts of conclusions and ideas, and differed about what the Prophet ﷺ wanted.

This means that if there was a verse that explicitly discusses the issue, they would have also interpreted it in their own way.

After all, the Prophet ﷺ explicitly said, "Whoever accepts me as his master, 'Alī is his master." Could he have been any clearer?

---

[115] Sūrat al-Mā'ida, verse 3.

[116] Arabic translator's note]: Some *sīra* books state that the Prophet ﷺ went out with 'Alī ؑ to seek forgiveness for those buried in al-Baqī' after Allah ﷻ ordered him to do so, whereas other sources mention that the Prophet ﷺ went out with his servant Abū Muwayhiba.

There is a difference between neglecting a *ḥadīth* although it is very explicit and between neglecting and abandoning a verse in the Qur'ān that explicitly mentions Imām ʿAlī's ﷺ name on the first day after the Prophet ﷺ passes away. [The author is referring to the historically proven neglect of the Prophet's ﷺ *ḥadīths* that mentioned ʿAlī ﷺ explicitly. The people abandoned these *ḥadīths* and headed to al-Saqīfa. Any verse that had explicitly mentioned Imām ʿAlī's ﷺ name would have met the same fate. The calamity would've been much greater in such a case].

In my preface to *Khilāfat va-vilāyat,* I mentioned that during the time of Imām ʿAlī ﷺ, a Jewish man wanted to reproach the Muslims and blame them for the incidents of the formative period of Islam—and they were blameworthy incidents indeed. The man told Imām ʿAlī ﷺ,[117] "As soon as you buried your Prophet ﷺ, you disagreed about him." Imām ʿAlī ﷺ had a wonderful reply: "We only disagreed about what he said and not about him. As for you, as soon as the water of the sea dried off of your feet, you told your prophet, 'make for us a god like the gods that they have.' He said, 'You are indeed an ignorant lot.'"[118]

Imām ʿAlī ﷺ meant to say that we did not disagree about our Prophet ﷺ himself but about an order that he gave us. As for you, the first thing you did was ask your Prophet ﷺ to forgo monotheism, your only principle of faith. In other words, we did not disagree about our Prophet ﷺ; we only disagreed about the meaning and significance of what he told us.

There is a big difference. The acts of certain people were interpreted in a certain way that is contrary to reality. It's one thing

[117] *Nahj al-Balāgha,* saying 317.

[118] [English translator's note]: Sūrat al-Aʿrāf, verse 138.

to misinterpret the Prophet's ﷺ words. Abandoning a verse that was very explicit and or distorting the Qur'ān is a different thing entirely.

Question: I would like to rephrase the question that the doctor [the previous asker] asked this way. It's true that the Qur'ān follows the methodology of explaining principles only. However, an issue as exceptionally important as succession and government in Islam should've been mentioned explicitly and in detail in the Qur'ān. I don't even mean simply mentioning names. I mean that it should've been revealed to the Prophet ﷺ, for instance, that he had to appoint his successor and that successor had to appoint his successor and so on. Alternatively, the Qur'ān should've stated whether the successor should be appointed by consultation or election.

This issue, as far as I know, was left ambiguous in the Qur'ān. In all cases, we do not have an explicit specific methodology. That's one point. Another point relates to a book I read a while ago about government in Islam. The book contained many sayings by Imām ʿAlī ؑ and others that stated that succession was an affair that concerned the Muslims, and the Muslims had to reach a conclusion about it. Imām ʿAlī ؑ wanted to say that the matter of succession does not concern me alone; it depends on the consultation and opinion of the Muslims.

This book actually contained many proofs that support the view that government in Islam is an electoral issue; it does not depend on one individual that appoints the successor that he prefers.

I would like to know your opinion about these matters.

The third point is this. Let us suppose that these twelve Imāms appointed their successors one after the other through revelation or any other way. What is the obligation of the Islamic society after the twelve Imāms concerning the principle of choosing and designating the successor? I'm not talking about the mode of designation. Is there a text stating that revelation stipulates twelve Imāms who have certain characteristics like infallibility and so on, and then the caliphate becomes a matter of election during the age of occultation? Is there such a declaration or not? We believe in the necessity of the government of a *mujtahid* who possesses all the qualifications (*jāmiʿ lil-shurūṭ*), but this is an act of *ijtihād* on our behalf because the twelfth Imām is absent. However, it should be up to the Qurʾān to set a primary, mandatory, practical program that states that the government after the Prophet ﷺ is limited to a number of infallibles. After that, the government is left to the *ummah*, and it will have to elect the ruler based on consultation. Alternatively, the program could state that the government should go to the jurist.

This issue remained suspended without a solution after the reign of the eleventh Imām ؑ, which surrounded it with many problems, views, and theories. My question is this: how can this issue be resolved from our point of view as Shīʿa?

Answer: We went over some of these issues in our past sessions. It seems that you too are limiting the issue to the government alone.

In the past weeks we pointed out that the issue of government is distinct from the Imamate. The issue of government during the time of the Imām is like the Prophet's ؑ government from the Shīʿa's point of view. It's an exceptional issue.

Just as no one wonders about the obligation of government in the presence of the Prophet ﷺ, it also becomes secondary and marginal in the presence of the Imām for the Shīʿa.

If we wanted to address the issue of the government separately, this may be done if there was no Imām (and such a time does not exist) or if he was hidden from sight. Naturally, this is a very important issue. In this light, we don't deny the principle of "and their affairs are by counsel among themselves,"[119] but what does the consultation concern? Does it apply to the text of the Qur'ān that expresses clear obligations? Consultation has no place in cases like this; it applies to things that do not have divine rulings and specific commands.

As for the book *al-Ḥukūma fil-Islām,* I did not fully look into it, but unfortunately, it seems to be a biased book to a great degree. It only mentioned some proofs and turned a blind eye to the proofs that contradict them; this is a big flaw. If a person wants to write, he should include all the available proofs then choose among them and give appropriate importance to each one accordingly. Another flaw is that it takes things out of context. I haven't personally read this book but I'm relating the opinion of experts who have. It cuts off the beginnings and endings of texts and jumps right into the middle, which conveys a different meaning than the meaning of the text as a unified whole. In addition, a large part of the matters discussed in the book relate to the time of the presence of the Imām and not to the Imamate itself. If they weren't related to the time of the presence of the Imām, it would be a different matter.Lesson Five: Duties and Responsibilities of the Prophets

[119] Sūrat al-Shūrā, verse 38.

The Imamate in the Qur᾿ān

Our discussion in the previous session revolved around the verse "Today I have perfected your religion for you, and I have completed My blessing upon you, and I have approved Islam as your religion." [120]We said that the internal proofs of the verse itself agree with the external proofs, i.e. Sunni and Shīʿī reports. These reports proved that the verse was about Ghadīr Khumm.

Since our discussion is about relevant Qur᾿ānic verses that the Shīʿa use to prove the Imamate, I thought it would be a good idea to point out other verses that Shīʿī scholars rely on in order to properly present their methodology.

Of these verses is another verse in Sūrat al-Mā᾿ida that comes about sixty verses after "Today I have perfected your religion."[121] It is the verse where Allah ﷻ says, "O Prophet! Communicate that which has been sent down to you from your Lord, and if you do not, you will not have communicated His message, and Allah shall protect you from the people."[122]

Before we begin our discussion, it is necessary to begin with a preface that will help me to clarify the idea we spoke of when discussing the previous verse.

The Uniqueness of the Verses on Ahl al-Bayt

The really puzzling issue is that the verses that concern Ahl al-Bayt —or at least the ones that are specific to Imām ʿAlī ؑ from our point of view as Shīʿa—are unique. Although these verses contain internal proofs and pieces of evidence that prove their relation to

---

[120] Sūrat al-Mā᾿ida, verse 3.

[121] Sūrat al-Mā᾿ida, verse 3.

[122] Sūrat al-Mā᾿ida, verse 67.

Ahl al-Bayt, it seems that there is a tendency to convey this central idea in the verse through other ideas or contexts that override the main idea and lead it to being neglected.

Muḥammad Taqī Sharīʿatī explained this idea rather well at the beginning of his *Khilāfat va-vilāyat.* Others have doubtlessly referred to this issue, but Muḥammad Taqī Sharīʿatī's work is the first of its kind in Persian. The question that arises is this: what's the secret behind these verses?

In context of answering this question, the answer to why Allah ﷻ didn't explicitly mention Imām ʿAlī's ؑ name in the Qurʾān if He wanted to designate him as the Prophet's ﷺ successor will become clear.

The Purification Verse

As an example, there is a verse known as the purification verse in which Allah ﷻ says, "Indeed Allah desires to repel all impurity from you, O People of the Household, and purify you with a thorough purification."[123] If we examine the verse, its meaning is very clear, as it states that Allah ﷻ wanted Ahl al-Bayt to be pure and elevated.

Allah's ﷻ saying, "purify you with a thorough purification" signifies a special kind of purification. It does not signify customary or medical purification such that He meant the purification of Ahl al-Bayt's bodies of diseases and germs.

I don't want to say that these things aren't included, but the definite kind of purification that's meant in the verse is primarily purification from the things that the Qurʾān itself labeled as

[123] Sūrat al-Aḥzāb, verse 33.

impurities (*rijs*). The terms impurity (*rijs*) and plague (*rijz*) include everything that is prohibited in the Qur'ān and every kind of sin, whether they are doctrinal, ethical, or practical. All these sins are impure and foul.

This is why it is said that the verse proves the infallibility of Ahl al-Bayt or their elevation from all forms of impurities and grave sins (*mūbiqāt*).

Let us pretend that we are not Sunnis or Shīʿa but that we are Christian Orientalists who came from the heartland of the Christian world to learn what the Book of the Muslims says. When we view this verse and then look at history, the Prophetic *sunnah* , and the body of *ḥadīth*, we will realize that the Shīʿa, who are loyal to Ahl al-Bayt to the exclusion of all others, aren't alone in tying the verse to Ahl al-Bayt. Even the groups that do not have a special connection to Ahl al-Bayt mention in their most trustworthy books that the verse was describing the Prophet's ﷺ household and that it was revealed on that famous occasion when the Prophet ﷺ came together with ʿAlī ؑ, al-Zahrā' ؑ, al-Ḥasan and al-Ḥusayn ؑ.

Ahl al-Sunnah relate that the verse was revealed when Umm Salama, [124]one of the Prophet's ﷺ wives, asked whether she was of the Ahl al-Bayt. The Prophet told her, "No, but you are on the path of the good." The sources of this *ḥadīth* are not one or two; many Sunni sources narrate this.

However, despite its clarity, this verse comes in the context of other verses that speak of the Prophet's ﷺ wives. The verse that precedes it says, "O wives of the Prophet! You are not like any other

---

124 The Shīʿa hold this lady in great reverence. They consider her the most revered wife of the Prophet ﷺ after Khadīja ؓ. The Sunnis respect her too, and consider her the third in importance after Khadīja and ʿĀ'isha.

women."[125] The verse doesn't aim to give special privileges but to explain that a sin committed by one of the Prophet's ﷺ wives warrants a double punishment because it's a twofold sin. The first sin is disobedience and the second is violating the sanctity of her husband the Prophet ﷺ. Similarly, her reward is doubled for these same reasons.

The same thing applies to Sayyids [descendants of the Prophet ﷺ] as well. They get double the punishment for disobedience and grave sins and double the reward for obedience and good deeds. For example, if a Sayyid drank alcohol, he would have committed two sins: the sin of having alcohol and the sin of violating the Prophet's ﷺ sanctity because he is related to him. Obviously, such a public act performed against the Prophet ﷺ by his own son would have a certain effect on others.

If we go back to the verses, we find that the pronoun in all of them is feminine: "You are not like any other women: if you are wary [of Allah] (*in ittaqaytunna*)."[126] This means that the addressees in the verse are the Prophet's ﷺ wives.

However, shortly after, the masculine pronoun appears in the text when Allah ﷻ says, "Indeed Allah desires to repel all impurity from you [*ʿankum* and not *ʿankunna*], O People of the Household, and purify you with a thorough purification"[127] before returning to feminine pronouns again.

Since nothing occurs in the Qurʾān randomly, this means the following:

---

[125] Sūrat al-Aḥzāb, verse 34.

[126] Sūrat al-Aḥzāb, verse 34.

[127] Sūrat al-Aḥzāb, verse 33.

First, the talk here becomes about the People of the Household whereas the previous context was about the Prophet's ﷺ wives: "O wives of the Prophet!"[128] Second, based on that, the pronouns changed from the feminine to the masculine. That did not happen without a reason, randomly, or arbitrarily. The text must've intended to discuss another issue that was different from the issue in the previous verses. The verses before and after the purification verse explained the obligations and commands concerning the Prophet's ﷺ wives, and they contained an air of threat, fear, and hope. The command in the verse is obvious in Allah's ﷻ saying, "Stay in your houses and do not display your finery with the display of the former [days of] ignorance."[129] The text is commanding and threatening the Prophet's ﷺ wives and it implicitly places them in a state of fear and hope. It makes them hope for the reward of good deeds and fear the punishment of the bad.

The significance of the purification verse is different from the preceding and succeeding verses; it exceeds praise to speak of an elevation from sins and acts of disobedience and a purification from grave sins. The addressees in the purification verse are the People of the Household whereas the addressees in the preceding and succeeding verses are the Prophet's ﷺ wives. This is why the pronouns change: they were masculine in the purification verse and feminine in the rest of the text.

The thing that happened was that this verse that has a different significance was still included among those verses, disrupting their context. It is just like a parenthetical clause (*jumla muʿtariḍa*) that a speaker says and then goes back to his original topic.

---

[128] Sūrat al-Aḥzāb, verse 34.

[129] Sūrat al-Aḥzāb, verse 35.

This is actually the secret behind Ahl al-Bayt's insistence that the verses of the Qur'ān might discuss different things in their beginnings, middles, and endings. Their emphasis on the importance of the exegesis of the Qur'ān is because of such reasons.

In fact, our narrations and Imāms 🕮 are not alone in saying that the verse has different addressees and contexts than the verses before and after it, and that it concerns Ahl al-Bayt 🕮 who were involved in that famous incident. Ahl al-Sunnah also mention this in their narrations.

Another Example

The same thing happens with the verse "Today I have perfected your religion for you"[130] but in a more amazing way. The previous context is about marginal and mundane things such as "You are permitted animals of grazing livestock."[131] The following verses then list exceptions such as the animal strangled or beaten to death, and that which dies by falling or is gored to death. The verse suddenly turns to "Today the faithless have despaired of your religion. So do not fear them, but fear Me. Today I have perfected your religion for you, and I have completed My blessing upon you, and I have approved Islam as your religion"[132] before going back to the previous context.[133]

---

[130] Sūrat al-Mā'ida, verse 3.

[131] Sūrat al-Mā'ida, verse 1.

[132] Sūrat al-Mā'ida, verse 3.

[133] [Arabic translator's note]: This means Allah ﷻ saying, "But should anyone be compelled by hunger, without inclining to sin, then Allah is indeed all-forgiving, all-merciful" (Sūrat al-Mā'ida, verse 3) then going back to "They ask you as to what is lawful to them" (Sūrat al-Mā'ida, verse 4).

It becomes clear that the text of "Today the faithless have despaired of your religion"[134] is not consistent with what comes before and after it. This means that it was included within a different topic and conveyed through it.

The verse that we are discussing today follows the same logic. It came in a way that if we removed it, the context of the other verse would not be disrupted, just like the verse "Today I have perfected your religion for you."[135]

The verses in question come amid other verses, but they cannot be said to be a continuation of what came before them or a preface to what is coming after them. They discuss a different topic, which is proved from the internal evidence in the verse as well as the narrations that both the Sunnis and the Shīʿa transmitted.

Since these verses are special and differ from the rest of the context, this means they were included among other unrelated verses. There must be a secret behind this matter, so what is it?

The Secret of the Matter

We can uncover this secret using the verse itself as well as the narrations of our Imāms ﷺ. The significance of this secret is that there are no Islamic rulings and teachings that were more poorly applied than the ones related to Ahl al-Bayt ﷺ and the Imamate of the Commander of the Believers ﷺ.

---

[134] Sūrat al-Māʾida, verse 3.

[135] Sūrat al-Māʾida, verse 3.

The poor commitment to this matter goes back to the Arabs' prejudice (*aṣabiyya*), which led to limited readiness to accept the idea of Ahl al-Bayt's ﷺ uniqueness.

Although the noble Prophet ﷺ received a divine order to appoint ʿAlī ﷺ, he was always on his guard against the hypocrites that the Qurʾān constantly mentioned. He feared their reaction and the possibility that they would say, according to the common expression, that he was simply looking out for himself . This is although the Prophet's ﷺ philosophy in life was that he did nothing for his own benefit. His own morals and the rulings of Islam both dictated that he should refrain from anything that gives him special privileges and distinguishes him from others.

This commitment was a huge factor in the success of the Prophet ﷺ.

Letting the *ummah* know that ʿAlī ﷺ was the Prophet's ﷺ successor was based on a divine command. Despite this, the Prophet ﷺ knew that if he did it, many people with little faith would interpret his act as an instance of personal privilege.[136]

When we go back to the verse "Today I have perfected your religion for you,"[137] we find that it was preceded by "Today the faithless have despaired of your religion. So do not fear them, but fear Me."[138] This means that the faithless knew that it was now pointless to oppose Islam after it became firmly established: "So do not fear them, but fear Me."[139] Fear Me because if inner strife strikes you, I will take the blessing of Islam away based on the divine *sunnah* of taking away the blessings of any people who changed their ways.

This "fear Me" means fear for yourselves because of yourselves. This means that the source of the fear is internal and not external. We also know that this verse belongs to Sūrat al-Mā'ida, which is the last *sūra* revealed to the Prophet ﷺ. This means that the verse

---

[136] [Arabic translator's note]: This was not simply an analysis or intuition. It was something that was actually said. An example is the verse "An asker asked for a punishment bound to befall—which none can avert from the faithless" (Sūrat al-Ma'ārij, verse 1). The story of this verse is that after the Prophet ﷺ called for the people to gather in Ghadīr Khumm, he took 'Alī's ؑ hand and said, "Whoever accepts me as his master, 'Alī is his master." The news spread far and wide, reaching al-Ḥārith b. al-Nu'mān al-Fihrī, who came to the Prophet ﷺ on a she-camel until he reached the region of al-Abtaḥ. Al-Ḥārith dismounted his she-camel, make it kneel, and tied it. He came to the Prophet ﷺ who was with a group of his companions and said, "O Muḥammad, you gave us Allah's command to testify that there is no god but Allah and that you are His Prophet ﷺ, and we accepted. You commanded us to pray five times a day and we accepted. You commanded us to give *zakāt* and we accepted. You commanded us to fast for a month and we accepted. You commanded us to perform the pilgrimage and we accepted. And yet that was not enough for you, so distinguished your own cousin and raised him above us and said, 'Whoever accepts me as his master, 'Alī is his master.' Did that come from you or from Allah?" The Prophet ﷺ answered, "By Allah who is the only god, it came from Allah." al-Ḥārith b. al-Nu'mān headed toward his mount while he was saying, "O Allah, if what he said was the truth, rain upon us stones from heaven or punish us with a painful punishment." When he reached his mount, a stone from Allah ﷻ fell on him, entering through his head and coming out of his behind. The stone killed him, and Allah ﷻ revealed the above verse about him. See *al-Kashf wal-tibyān*, 213.

[137] Sūrat al-Mā'ida, verse 3.

[138] Sūrat al-Mā'ida, verse 3.

[139] Sūrat al-Mā'ida, verse 3.

itself was revealed in the last two or three months of the Prophet's ﷺ life after Islam became strong and firmly established.

The same thing occurs in the other verses; the fear always came from the Muslims themselves and not from outside forces. Allah ﷻ says, "O Prophet! Communicate that which has been sent down to you from your Lord, and if you do not, you will not have communicated His message, and Allah shall protect you from the people." [140]

There is no other verse in the Qur᾽ān that urged the Prophet ﷺ to do something except this one. It's like when you want to encourage someone to do something that he is afraid of, and he hesitates.

This verse commands the Prophet ﷺ to communicate what was revealed to him. It involves warning, encouragement, and consolation. The point of this warning is that if you don't communicate what has been sent down to you, all your efforts to communicate the message would be for nothing. On the other hand, the verse is consoling the Prophet ﷺ and telling him not to fear the people: "and Allah shall protect you from the people." [141]

Let's go back to the verse "Today the faithless have despaired of your religion."[142] The Prophet ﷺ naturally did not fear the faithless, but the other verse "O Prophet! Communicate that which has been sent down to you from your Lord"[143] reveals that the Prophet ﷺ

[140] Sūrat al-Mā᾽ida, verse 67.

[141] Sūrat al-Mā᾽ida, verse 67.

[142] Sūrat al-Mā᾽ida, verse 3.

[143] Sūrat al-Mā᾽ida, verse 67.

was worried about the hypocrites. The cause of this worry was Islamic society itself.

I'm not concerned with that group of people that refused the caliphate of 'Alī ﷺ at the moment. I don't care if those people were internally faithless or not. What I do care about is the result: those people were simply not willing to accept the caliphate of 'Alī ﷺ.

Historical Proofs

When we reflect on the trajectory of historical events and consider the reality of the community, we find that it expresses this conclusion as well. 'Umar stated that they did not choose 'Alī ﷺ for the caliphate "out of fear for Islam" because the people did not accept him and listen to him.[144]

On another occasion, 'Umar went into discussion with 'Abd Allāh b. 'Abbās. 'Umar said that Quraysh refused Imām 'Alī ﷺ because they disliked the prospect that this particular house of Banū Hāshim would have both prophethood and the caliphate. It could not bear

144 [Arabic translator's note]: Nothing is more indicative of the author's words than historical facts themselves. These facts point out that a dialogue on the caliphate and Imām 'Alī's ﷺ right took place. Ibn 'Abbās mentioned that the Prophet ﷺ left the caliphate to 'Alī ﷺ before his death. 'Umar responded by saying, "The Prophet spoke some about 'Alī in a way that does not support a certain position or refute people's excuses. The Prophet was testing the *ummah* through 'Alī for a time. In his last illness, he wanted to explicitly mention 'Alī's name but I stood in the way because I feared for Islam. By Allah, Quraysh would never unanimously agree about 'Alī ﷺ. If he does assume this position, the Arabs would jump up in protest from every quarter. The Prophet ﷺ knew that I knew his intention, so he held his peace, and Allah hated the happening of anything other than what He willed." See *Sharḥ Nahj al-Balāgha*, 3/97.

seeing such a thing. Ibn ʿAbbās gave a very seasoned response, and used verses of the Qurʾān as proof.[145]

This was a reflection of the situation of Islamic society at the time, which was expressed in different ways. The Qurʾān expressed it in its own way, ʿUmar expressed it in his own way, and others expressed it in their own way when they said that they have to avenge their notables from ʿAlī ﷺ because he killed many of them in battle. The Arabs never forgave ʿAlī ﷺ for this given their vengeful characters, and they never forgot their killed fathers and brothers. Their response was refusing his caliphate and considering him unfit for them.

---

145 [Arabic translator's note]: It will be apparent to anyone who reviews Islamic history that ʿUmar often had conversations with Ibn ʿAbbās about the state of affairs and the issue of the caliphate. In one conversation, which the author is alluding to, ʿUmar asked Ibn ʿAbbās, "O Ibn ʿAbbās, do you know why the people refused you [Banū Hāshim]?" Ibn ʿAbbās said, "No, O Commander of the Believers." ʿUmar replied, "But I do." Ibn ʿAbbās asked, "Why is that?" ʿUmar said, "Quraysh loathed for you to have both prophethood and the caliphate lest you treat people with disdain. Quraysh viewed things, chose, and was guided and right." Ibn ʿAbbās asked, "Would the Commander of the Believers hear a complaint that I have?" ʿUmar, "Speak as you wish." Ibn ʿAbbās said, "As for the Commander of the Believers' saying that 'Quraysh loathed...' Allah ﷻ said of a people, 'That is because they loathed what Allah ﷻ has sent down, so He made their works fail' (Sūrat Muḥammad, verse 9). As for your saying that we would've been disdainful, if we wanted to be disdainful because of the caliphate, we would've been disdainful because of our kinship to the Prophet first. However, we are a people whose characters are like the character of the Prophet, to whom Allah ﷻ said, 'and indeed you possess a great character' (Sūrat al-Qalam, verse 4) and 'and lower your wing to the faithful' (Sūrat al-Ḥijr, verse 88). As for your saying, 'Quraysh chose,' Allah ﷻ says, 'Your Lord creates whatever He wishes and chooses. They have no choice.' You know, O Commander of the Believers, that Allah chose for this affair the person he chose. If Quraysh had viewed things the way Allah viewed them, then it would have been guided and right." ʿUmar said, "Be careful, Ibn ʿAbbās. Your hearts nursed an everlasting hatred and grudge against Quraysh." Ibn ʿAbbās said, "Be careful, Commander of the Believers. Don't attribute deceit to the hearts of Banū Hāshim, for their hearts are of the Prophet's ﷺ heart, which Allah purified. They are the Ahl al-Bayt about whom Allah said, "Indeed Allah desires to repel all impurity from you, O People of the Household, and purify you with a thorough purification" (Sūrat al-Aḥzāb, verse 33). As for your mentioning of grudges, how can someone not hold a grudge when a right of his was usurped and given to others?" to the end of this conversation that historians like al-Ṭabarī, Ibn al-Athīr, and Ibn Abī al-Ḥadīd mentioned. See *al-Kāmil fil tārīkh*, 3/62, *Sharḥ Nahj al-Balāgha*, 3/106.

Some of Ahl al-Sunnah held to this logic to justify their position. Even when they admitted that Imām 'Alī ﷺ was preferred over other candidates, their excuse was that he had many enemies.

This means that there was an atmosphere of anxiety from the time of the Prophet ﷺ about the refusal of Imām 'Alī's ﷺ Imamate.

Perhaps the secret behind the Qur'ān's style in these verses is that the proofs and clues in them enable any sound person who is not biased to understand their meaning. It seems that the Qur'ān did not want to express its purpose in a way that allowed those who were eager to rebel to be so obviously confrontational against Islam.

It was as though the purpose of this Qur'ānic style was to say, "The group that will rebel anyway should not be allowed to portray its rebellion as a direct and sharp refusal of the Qur'ān. Let it at least have a pretext that hides its real position."

This possibility explains why the purification verse was in the middle of those other verses. However, any intelligent and thoughtful person is able to understand that the purification verse is different from its context.

The same thing may be said about the verse "Today I have perfected your religion for you, and I have completed My blessing upon you, and I have approved Islam as your religion"[146] and "O Prophet! Communicate that which has been sent down to you from your Lord."[147]

---

[146] Sūrat al-Mā'ida, verse 3.

[147] Sūrat al-Mā'ida, verse 67.

Your Guardian is Only Allah

There are other verses that push a person to think and understand that there's something special going on. When a person relies on recurrent narrations, he will become certain of this fact.

One of these verses is "Your guardian is only Allah, His Prophet, and the faithful who maintain the prayer and give the *zakāt* while bowing down."[148] This verse contains a wonderful expression because giving *zakāt* while bowing down in prayer is not a required Islamic practice. The context indicates that the verse is pointing to a specific incident.[149]

The Qur'ān kept things vague out of caution about the aforementioned rebellion. If the people had rebelled against explicitly mentioned names, both friends and foes would have considered it a rebellion against the Qur'ān itself. For this reason, the Qur'ān used a metonymy that may be understood by any unbiased person to refer to a specific incident. The verse "who

---

[148] Sūrat al-Mā'ida, verse 55.

[149] In his *tafsīr*, al-Fakhr al-Rāzī said, "'Ikrima narrated from Ibn 'Abbās that the verse is about 'Alī. It was also narrated from 'Abd Allāh b. Salām that when this verse was revealed, he said, "O Prophet of Allah, I saw 'Alī giving away his ring to a needy person while bowing down, so we will take 'Alī as our guardian." It was narrated from Abū Dharr that he performed the noon prayer with the Prophet ﷺ one day. A needy person was begging in the mosque but no one gave him anything. The man raised his hands up to the sky and said, "Allah be my witness that I begged for help in the Prophet's Mosque and no one gave me anything." 'Alī was bowing in prayer so he extended his right-hand finger, which had a ring on it. The beggar came and took the ring. When the Prophet saw this, he said, "O Allah, my brother Mūsā asked you by saying, 'My Lord! Open my breast for me. Make my affair easy for me. Remove the hitch from my tongue, [so that] they may understand my discourse. Appoint for me a minister from my family, Aaron, my brother. Strengthen my back through him, and make him my associate in my affair,' and You responded, 'We will strengthen your arm by means of your brother and invest both of you with such authority.' O Allah, I am Your pure Prophet Muḥammad, so open my breast for me. Make my affair easy for me. Appoint for me a minister from my family, 'Alī, and strengthen my back through him." Abū Dharr said, "By Allah, the Prophet was barely done saying these words when Jibrā'īl descended and said, 'O Muḥammad, recite: 'Your guardian is only Allah, His Prophet, and the faithful who maintain the prayer and give the *zakāt* while bowing down.'" See al-Fakhr al-Rāzī, *al-Tafsīr al-kabīr*, 12/26.

maintain the prayer and give the *zakāt* while bowing down" does not reflect an ordinary situation; it points to an exceptional incident that took place. At this point, the question that arises is: what is this incident? We find that both the Sunnis and the Shī'a agreed that the verse was revealed about 'Alī 🕮.[150]

The Mystics' Words

If we reflect deeply on other verses, they further clarify this idea. There is something that the ancient mystics have mentioned. The Shī'a believe in it too, but the mystics expressed it beautifully. They say that the Imamate and guardianship are the internal dimension of the Sharia.

The meaning is that the person who gets to the heart of the matter is one who surpasses empty husks to reach the core. The Imamate and guardianship in Islam are both among the essential, core issues. This means that a person who reaches the core understands the Imamate and the guardianship. People have been invited to reach this core, but some of them get there and some of them do not. [151]

Now we will discuss other verses with the goal of knowing the nature of the Shī'a's proof and logic about the Imamate.

---

150 [Arabic translator's note]: We read in the commentary on this noble verse in *al-Durr al-Manthūr*: "al-Ṭabarānī in his *al-Awsaṭ*, and Ibn Mardawayh from 'Ammār b. Yāsir, mentioned the following. A beggar approached 'Alī while he was bowing down in voluntary prayer, so he took off his ring and gave it to the man. The Prophet came and was informed of this, and the verse 'Your guardian is only Allah, His Prophet, and the faithful who maintain the prayer and give the *zakāt* while bowing down' was revealed. The Prophet recited it to his companions and said, 'Whoever accepts me as his master, 'Alī is his master. O Allah, be a guardian for whoever accepts him as master and be an enemy for his enemy.'" See al-Sayūṭī, *al-Durr al-Manthūr*, 2/293.

151 [Arabic translator's note]: The author casually and vaguely mentioned that the Imamate and guardianship are internal dimensions of the Sharia without further clarification. The reason is that the text was originally a lecture and not a written research project. To look into some simple and elaborate works on this idea, see al-'Allāma al-Ṭabāṭabā'ī, *Kitāb al-Shī'a*, 204ff (Arabic translation), idem., *Risālat al-wilāya* (Arabic translation), Shahīd Murtaḍā Muṭahharī, *al-Walā' wal-wilāya*, trans. Ja'far Ṣādiq al-Khalīlī (Mu'assasat al-Bi'tha).

The Imamate and Prophethood for the Shīʿa

There is a marvelous verse in the Qurʾān that comes in the context of certain verses about the Imamate. This verse does not concern ʿAlī b. Abī Ṭālib 🌼 but rather the issue of the Imamate itself. It features a concept that I already spoke of and will speak of again.

I mentioned before that the Muslim theologians of old made a big mistake when they asked about the conditions of the Imamate. Such an inquiry implies that the Sunnis accept the Imamate just as we Shīʿa do. This makes it sound like the difference is merely about the conditions of the Imamate: we believe in infallibility and designation and they do not.

The truth is that the Sunnis do not believe in our form of the Imamate at all. The Imamate they believe in concerns the worldly dimension, which is only one of the affairs of the Imamate for us.

An example of this is reflected in the issue of prophethood. One of the Prophet's 🌼 responsibilities was to rule the Muslims, but that does not mean that prophethood is equivalent to rulership and governance. Prophethood includes thousands of responsibilities. However, as we mentioned before, in the presence of the Prophet 🌼, the Muslims simply do not need another ruler because the Prophet 🌼 is the ruler.

The Sunnis say that the Imamate means government, and the Imām means the ruler of the Muslims. This means that the Imām is a person whom the Muslims should elect to rule them.

This means that Ahl al-Sunnah limited the Imamate to the government.

As for the Shīʿa, the Imamate for them is second only to prophethood, and it is even more elevated than some degrees of prophethood. The *ulū al-ʿazm* are the prophets who possessed the rank of prophet and Imām. Many prophets weren't Imāms, but the *ulū al-ʿazm* reached the rank of Imamate eventually.

We don't ask about the identity of the ruler when a Prophet ﷺ is present because a Prophet ﷺ transcends the human dimension. In the same way, it is meaningless to look for another person to rule in the presence of the Imām ؑ. Talking about this issue can be objectively explained in the absence of the Imām (if we assume that he does not exist or is absent as is the case of our time).

We should be careful about confusing the Imamate with the issue of government and then wondering about our position and the position of Ahl al-Sunnah. The Imamate is different from the government . For the Shīʿa, it is a phenomenon and a concept that equals prophethood at its highest levels.

We can conclude from the above that the difference between the Sunnis and the Shīʿa is that we believe in the Imamate while the Sunnis do not believe in it at all. It's not that they believe in it but differ with us about the conditions of the Imām.

The Imamate in the Descendants of Ibrāhīm

The verse that we now want to discuss relates to the concept of the Imamate as the Shīʿa understand it. The Shīʿa believe that this verse reflects a dimension of the Imamate that was not limited to the period following the Prophet's ؑ passing. This dimension goes back to the time of previous prophets ؑ, and it resides in the descendants of Ibrāhīm ؑ until the Day of Judgment.

The verse I mean is "And when his Lord tested Abraham with certain words, and he fulfilled them, He said, 'I am making you the Imam of mankind.' Said he, 'And from among my descendants?' He said, 'My pledge does not extend to the unjust.'"[152]

Ibrāhīm Tested

The Qur'ān spoke about the tribulations of Ibrāhīm ﵇ and his steadfastness in the face of Namrūd. It spoke about how he ﵇ was willing to be burned with fire in his steadfastness and related the rest of the incidents that he went through.

One of the things he ﵇ went through was an astonishing thing that no person could bear except if he surrendered to Allah ﷻ and worshiped Him absolutely.

In his old age, Ibrāhīm ﵇ was given a firstborn from his wife Hājar, who was seventy or eighty, after a lifetime without descendants. At that moment, Ibrāhīm ﵇ received an order to leave Shām and Syria and head toward Hijaz. He had to leave his wife and son alone there. No logic could justify this except the logic of absolute surrender [to Allah]. This was a command of Allah ﷻ, which Ibrāhīm ﵇ felt through revelation, and it had to be obeyed. Allah ﷻ tells us that Ibrāhīm ﵇ said, "Our Lord! I have settled part of my descendants in a barren valley, by Your sacred House, our Lord, that they may maintain the prayer."[153]

Ibrāhīm ﵇ knew where things were headed through divine revelation, but he emerged from this test in the best state possible.

---

[152] Sūrat al-Baqara, verse 124.

[153] Sūrat Ibrāhīm, verse 37.

Sacrificing the Son

The second test that was even harder than the first was the command to sacrifice his son. Ibrāhīm ﷺ received an order to sacrifice his son by his own hand at Minā, where we now commemorate that ultimate surrender of his by offering sacrifices ourselves.

After he received the command two and three times in the form of dreams, he was certain that it was really divine revelation. He spoke to his son about it, and the son submissively and without argument said, "Father! Do whatever you have been commanded. If Allah wishes, you will find me to be patient."[154]

The Qur'ān depicts the scene beautifully when it says, "So when they had both submitted [to Allah's will], and he had laid him down on his forehead..."[155] It means that they went through with the command and Ibrāhīm ﷺ did not have the slightest doubt that he would have to sacrifice his own son, just as Ismā'īl ﷺ was certain that he was going to be sacrificed. When they both did their parts with absolute peace and certainty, the call came: "We called out to him, 'O Abraham! You have indeed fulfilled the vision!"[156]

This means that the purpose was not sacrificing Ismā'īl ﷺ and decapitating him. The Qur'ān did not mention a new command that forbade Ibrāhīm ﷺ from the act, but it said, "You have indeed fulfilled the vision!"[157] It means: "By practically complying with what was asked of you, it is now over." This is because, like I said,

154 Sūrat al-Ṣāffāt, verse 102-103.

155 Sūrat al-Ṣāffāt, verse 103.

156 Sūrat al-Ṣāffāt, verse 104.

157 Sūrat al-Ṣāffāt, verse 104.

the goal was never to sacrifice Ismāʿīl 🕮, but rather the expression of submission and surrender by both father and son, and this was what truly happened.

The Qurʾānic text is clear in stating that Ibrāhīm 🕮 was given descendants in his old age. When the angels came to give him tidings of a son, his wife asked, "Oh, my! Shall I, an old woman, bear [children], and [while] this husband of mine is an old man?!"[158] The angels said to her, "They said, 'Are you amazed at Allah's dispensation? [That is] Allah's mercy and His blessings upon you, members of the household."[159]

Ibrāhīm 🕮 had descendants as an old man when he was already a prophet. There are many verses in the Qurʾān about Ibrāhīm 🕮, but their point is that he was given descendants at the old age of seventy or eighty after he became a prophet. He remained alive for one or two decades after that, until Isḥāq and Ismāʿīl 🕮 had grown. Ismāʿīl 🕮 was even old enough to assist him in building the Kaʿba.

The verse "And when his Lord tested Abraham with certain words, and he fulfilled them, He said, 'I am making you the Imam of mankind.' Said he, 'And from among my descendants?' He said, 'My pledge does not extend to the unjust'"[160] reveals that the Imamate was given to Ibrāhīm 🕮 after he passed the tests that he went through. When was that and what period does the verse concern? It is certainly not related to the time before Ibrāhīm's 🕮 prophethood because it mentions revelation which is a characteristic of prophethood.

---

[158] Sūrat Hūd, verse 72.

[159] Sūrat Hūd, verse 73.

[160] Sūrat al-Baqara, verse 124

This means it relates to the period of his prophethood, but do we mean the beginning of his prophethood? No, it relates to a later stage of his prophethood for two reasons. First, it explicitly speaks of tests, and all the tests that Ibrāhīm ﷺ went through took place during his prophethood. In addition, the most important of these tests took place during the later part of his prophethood. Second, the verse mentions descendants, which means that Ibrāhīm ﷺ already had descendants at the time.

This means that this verse is telling Ibrāhīm ﷺ: you will be given an additional merit in the final years of your life and a separate position [other than prophethood because he was already a prophet]. This position was expressed in Allah's ﷻ saying, "I am making you the Imam of mankind."[161] It's clear that Ibrāhīm ﷺ was already a messenger and a prophet before this new bounty. He reached one stage after another, except one that he could only reach after he passed all the other divine tests.[162]

Doesn't all this point to a separate concept in the Qur'ān called the Imamate?

And now, what does the Imamate mean?

The Imamate is the Pledge of Allah

The Imamate means reaching the level of the Perfect Man who becomes an example for mankind. When Ibrāhīm ﷺ was given the

---

161 Sūrat al-Baqara, verse 124.

162 [Arabic translator's note]: A noble *ḥadīth* states the following: "Allah made Ibrāhīm a servant before he made him a prophet, and He made him a prophet before He made him a messenger, and He made him a messenger before He made him His friend, and He made him His friend before He made him an Imām. When He combined all these merits for him, He said, 'I am making you the Imam of mankind.' Ibrāhīm knew it was such a great thing, which was why he made the request: 'And from among my descendants?'" See *al-Kāfī*, 1/175, *ḥadīth* 2.

Imamate, he ﷵ immediately thought of his descendants. The answer he received was: "My pledge does not extend to the unjust."[163]

This verse referred to the Imamate as Allah's ﷻ pledge. This is why we as Shīʿa believe that the Imamate is something that is connected to Allah ﷻ. The Qurʾān itself attributes it to Allah ﷻ when He says, "My pledge."[164] It is not a regular pledge that concerns people. When we realize that the Imamate is not the same thing as the government, we will not be surprised to learn that it is something connected to Allah ﷻ.

Someone might ask, "Is the government related to Allah or the people?" To this person we say that the government that he is asking about is something other than the Imamate. The Imamate is Allah's ﷻ pledge, and Allah's ﷻ pledge is not extended to the unjust among Ibrāhīm's ﷵ descendants. The Qurʾān did not respond to Ibrāhīm's ﷵ question with absolute negation or confirmation. It distinguished between two segments of Ibrāhīm's ﷵ descendants. Since it excluded the unjust from this pledge, this means that it kept the just included. This verse indicates that the Imamate has remained with Ibrāhīm's ﷵ descendants in general.

---

163 Sūrat al-Baqara, verse 124.

164 Sūrat al-Baqara, verse 124.

Another Verse

There is another verse in the Qur'ān that also mentions Ibrāhīm ﷺ. In this verse, Allah ﷻ says, "And He made it a lasting word among his posterity."[165] This verse is proof that the Imamate is a reality that will remain among Ibrāhīm's ﷺ descendants.

The Identity of the Unjust

The verse mentions the unjust. When the Imāms ﷺ wanted to prove that someone was unjust, they would rely on this verse. The question that arises is this: who is meant by the word "unjust"?

The unjust, in the Qur'ān, is every person who inflicts injustice upon himself or others. According to social custom, the unjust is anyone who transgresses the rights of others, whereas the Qur'ān generalizes the concept to include transgressing others' and one's own rights as well. There are many verses in the Qur'ān that speak of wronging oneself.

Al-'Allāma al-Ṭabāṭabā'ī mentions the words of one of his teachers about Ibrāhīm's ﷺ request concerning his descendants. He says that there are the following possibilities about the righteousness and corruption of these descendants. The first possibility is that these descendants have always been unjust throughout their lives. The second possibility is that these descendants were unjust at first and then they became righteous. The third possibility is that these descendants were righteous at first and then they became corrupt. The fourth possibility is that these descendants have never been unjust.

---

165 Sūrat al-Zukhruf, verse 28.

Al-ʿAllāma al-Ṭabāṭabāʾī says that it is impossible for Ibrāhīm ﷺ to request such a lofty thing such as the Imamate, which was given to him after being a prophet and a messenger, for his descendants who have been unjust throughout their lives. It is also impossible for him to request it for his descendants who were righteous at first and then became corrupt.

This means that Ibrāhīm ﷺ requested the Imamate for the righteous among his descendants. This group is divided into two categories. The first includes those who have always been righteous, and the second includes those who were unjust but became righteous. Since Ibrāhīm ﷺ limited his request to these two categories, this might mean that his request includes those who had been tarnished with injustice in the past and became righteous later. However, the Qurʾān itself says, "My pledge does not extend to the unjust."[166] It is denying the Imamate to those who had committed injustice in the past. Since the Qurʾān denies the Imamate to those who had been unjust but became righteous, those who are actually unjust are automatically excluded, whether they have always been unjust or whether they were righteous but later became unjust.

This means that the Qurʾān is denying the Imamate of anyone who has ever committed injustice. [Imām al-Riḍā ﷺ says, "This verse invalidated the Imamate of every unjust person until the Day of Judgment"].[167]

This is the Shīʿa's proof of the impossibility of anyone's Imamate if they spent a portion of their life as polytheists.

---

166 Sūrat al-Baqara, verse 124.

167 [Arabic translator's note]: *al-Kāfī*, 1/199.

Audience Q and A

Question: What does the concept of "infallible" mean? Is it the product of our own logic as Shī'a, meaning that we created it? Does it already have established principles that we only cultivated and arranged? Does the word "infallible" apply to a person who does not sin or should this person never be mistaken as well?

Twenty years ago, I used to attend the lessons of the late Mīrzā Abū al-Ḥasan Khān Furūghī. He had researched the concept of infallibility and had a specific doctrine about it too. He spoke in a detailed and organized way. We didn't understand 80% of what he was saying, but of the 20% that we did understand, we could tell that he defined the concept of infallibility in a different way. He used to say that the infallible person was not someone who does not sin because there are many people who have never sinned throughout their lives and we don't call them infallible.

Actually, I'm not concerned about this logic at the moment because I'm sure Shaykh Muṭahharī has an answer about the meaning of infallible and infallibility. However, if we say that the infallible person is someone who is never mistaken, two of our twelve Imāms 🕊 actually assumed the caliphate, I mean by them Imām 'Alī 🕊 as well Imām al-Ḥasan 🕊 who assumed it for a very short time. What's certain is that they both were mistaken sometimes while assuming the caliphate and governing the land. From the angle of pure historical logic, there's nothing to make us hesitate about the occurrence of these mistakes. Naturally, mistakes are incongruent with the concept of infallibility.

For example, Imām al-Ḥasan 🕊 appointed 'Ubayd Allāh b. 'Abbās as the leader of the army fighting Mu'āwiya. Imām 'Alī 🕊 himself appointed 'Abd Allāh b. 'Abbās as governor over Baṣra. If Imām

ʿAlī ﷺ had known that ʿAbd Allāh b. ʿAbbās would be involved in that horrible scandal [stealing from the treasury of Baṣra], he definitely wouldn't have appointed him. This certainly means that when Imām ʿAlī ﷺ appointed him, he believed him to be the best candidate for the position. After he chose him, ʿAbd Allāh b. ʿAbbās committed that disgraceful act.

If we examine the period of Imām ʿAlī's ﷺ rule, we will find many other, historically sound examples. What I want to say is that these incidents don't conform with the definition of infallibility.

The benefit of research about the concept of infallibility is reduced if the research itself is unilateral and limited to a group of people who share the same convictions. If a person has a doctrine that he believes in and loves, human nature makes him averse to hearing anything that opposes it. This is all the more true for us Shīʿa because we are taught to love Shīʿism and the household of ʿAlī ﷺ from childhood. We've never heard criticisms about them.

Even more to the point, perhaps criticisms against Islam itself and its principles go down easier for us, including monotheism and servanthood to Allah ﷻ. However, we've never heard any criticism directed at Shīʿism and the Imāms ﷺ. In addition, a person hears about some incidents in the Imāms' ﷺ lives and is driven to wonder why they acted in this way and not that.

Based on these facts, it feels extremely wrong for us when a person accuses Imām al-Ḥasan ﷺ of making mistakes for example. The issue might become even more complicated if the accusation was directed at Imām al-Ḥusayn ﷺ.

For example, Shaykh Muṭahharī spoke about something in our first session and again today, which is the verse on those who "maintain the prayer and give the *zakāt* while bowing down."[168] He relied on it a lot because it only applies to Imām 'Alī ﷺ and his donation of his ring while bowing down. However, this proof does not seem very logical and reasonable to me for several reasons. One of them is what we know about Imām 'Alī's ﷺ absorption during prayer to the extent that he did not look at or recognize anyone. It was even mentioned that he did not recognize people passing right in front of him while doing his ablutions, so how about his prayers?

My question is if this is someone's state during prayer, how can he pay such attention to other people to the extent of noticing the needy person enter, beg, and be denied such that Imām 'Alī ﷺ finally took the ring out of his own finger and gave it to him?

Besides, giving poor people money is not such a great thing, and it's not so important at the personal level for a person to interrupt his prayers for it [meaning to interrupt his personal connection to Allah ﷻ for the purpose of giving *zakāt*].

Another reason that logically diminishes the value of this verse as a proof is that *zakāt* does not include rings. According to the legal opinions of Shī'ī jurists, rings are part of the *zakāt*.

In addition, some people have shown a certain bias in this regard to exaggerate the issue by saying that the ring that Imām 'Alī ﷺ gave away was a very expensive ring. However, we know Imām 'Alī ﷺ never wore expensive rings.

Answer: As for the asker's mention of the necessity of objections, this is indeed a beneficial thing that would enrich all of our sessions.

[168] Sūrat al-Mā'ida, verse 55

I can say nothing in response to this issue except by acknowledging that this is a good and beneficial thing indeed.

Concerning the meaning of infallibility, it might cause a person to think that Allah ﷻ particularly monitors a certain group of people, and as soon as they proceed to commit a sin, He forbids him immediately. However, this is certainly not what infallibility is. If that was the meaning of infallibility, it wouldn't have counted as a perfection. Let's suppose that someone is constantly watching a child and forbidding him from doing anything wrong. This would not count as proof of the child's perfection.

There is a further dimension of infallibility that may be inferred from the Qur'ān, and particularly from the story of prophet Yūsuf ﷺ and his trouble with that woman [Zulaykha]. The Qur'ān mentions that she approached him ﷺ: "She certainly made for him"[169] and that if he ﷺ didn't receive the proof of his Lord, he would've been inclined to her: "and he would have made for her [too] had he not beheld the proof of his Lord."[170]

The verse indicates that Yūsuf ﷺ was an ordinary human being, and a young man who had desires. The woman was inclined to him, but he was not responsive to her. He could've been inclined to her too if he didn't see the proof of his Lord. Yūsuf ﷺ had a perfect faith; it is the faith of witnessing (*īmān shuhūdī*) that makes the faults and harms of such a deed manifest. This faith that Allah ﷻ bestowed on Yūsuf ﷺ was what protected him and prevented him from getting involved in such an act.

---

[169] Sūrat Yūsuf, verse 24.

[170] Sūrat Yūsuf, verse 24.

Each of us has a degree of infallibility that guards us against certain slips and sins. This infallibility does not come from a preventative outside force but from our perfect faith about the danger of those slips and sins.

For example, I would not throw myself down the roof of a four-story building or plunge myself into a raging fire. Plunging myself into fire is a sin, but I would never do it because I am certain about its harms, which are manifest before me.

We can only commit such a sin (jumping from a height, going into a fire) if we overlook its dangers. A child, however, may extend his hand toward a fire. Why is that? It's because the danger of this sin is not manifest to him as it is manifest to us.

Moving on to the example of an upright person, his faculty of piety (*malakat al-taqwā*) prevents him from committing many sins. This faculty gives the person a degree of infallibility corresponding to it, meaning that he is as infallible as his faculty allows.

We conclude from what has been said that infallibility from a sin is related to a person's faith in the reality and danger of that sin. We accepted what the Sharia determined to be sins as an act of submission. We don't drink or gamble because Islam and the Sharia forbade these acts. Avoiding such practices is related to our awareness of their disadvantages. However, this awareness of ours is not as immediately manifest to us as our awareness of how dangerous it is to throw ourselves into a fire. If we believe in the danger of these sins as deeply as we believed in the danger of fire, we would become infallible.

This means that infallibility is the height and perfection of faith. The person who said, "If the veil were removed for me, my certainty would not have grown greater"[171] is definitely infallible. The dangers are equally manifest for him on both sides of the veil [i.e. between the worlds of the seen and the unseen]. For example, he feels that using swear words and harming people with them is like setting a scorpion loose on his own self. For this reason, he refrains from such an act. The Qur'ān itself pointed out similar degrees of faith. This means that infallibility is relative, having ranks and degrees.

The infallibles are free of acts that are considered sins for us, which we sometimes commit and sometimes avoid. They, on the other hand, are infallible and never commit such acts at all. However, the infallibles themselves have their own ranks and degrees; they are not identical. The infallibles also move from rank to rank; just as we lack infallibility from sins, they are not infallible at certain ranks.

They are infallible of what is considered a sin for us. What counts as a sin for them, however, is actually a good deed (*ḥasana*) for us because we haven't reached their level [the good deeds of the pious (*abrār*) are the bad deeds of those drawn near (*al-muqarrabūn*)."

For example, if a fifth grader solves a grade-six-level equation, that is an achievement that merits a reward. However, if a ninth grader solves the same equation, it is not a merit and does not have any value.

The things that we consider good deeds are bad deeds for infallible people. This explains the logic of the Qur'ān when it attributes sins to infallible people: "Adam disobeyed his Lord, and went amiss"[172] or "that Allah may forgive you what is past of your sin and what is

[171] *Safīnat al-biḥār*, 2/734. The saying is by Imām 'Alī ﷺ

[172] Sūrat Ṭāhā, verse 121.

to come."[173] Such verses indicate that infallibility is relative: an infallible has his own degree of infallibility and we have ours.

In other words, the extent of infallibility goes back to the degree and perfection of faith. At every degree of faith, a person necessarily has a degree of infallibility until he reaches the height of faith and perfection. He becomes necessarily infallible at the level of "had he not beheld the proof of his Lord."[174] This shows the error in thinking that an infallible person is a regular person like us who is always inclined to sin but Allah ﷻ commands an angel to prevent him from sinning and steers him away. If this were the case, there would be no difference between Imām ʿAlī ؑ and I because both of us are inclined to sin. The only difference would be that he has an angel assigned to him to forbid him from sinning whereas I don't!

If refraining from sinning happened through an external deterrent, there would be no virtue in it. It's as though someone else steals but I don't because I have a policeman constantly watching me. In this case, I would be as much a thief as he is with one difference between us. He steals because there is no policeman to prevent him, and I am a thief but the presence of the policeman prevents me from stealing. There is no virtue in that.

The primary facet of infallibility is infallibility from sins. Infallibility from mistakes is a different matter that has two dimensions. The first dimension is infallibility from making mistakes in communicating things from Allah ﷻ. Can we say the Prophet ﷺ explained the rulings to us but might've been mistaken? Might Allah ﷻ have revealed a ruling to him in one way but the Prophet explained it in another? An example is similar mistakes that we

[173] Sūrat al-Fatḥ, verse 2.

[174] Sūrat Yūsuf, verse 24.

make in this regard, such as when we are told to relay this message but we relay it in a different way. In such a case, we would have no confidence in the Prophet's ﷺ words because he might've made a mistake in communicating the message. This absolutely cannot be.

Concerning the other issues mentioned in the question, the esteemed engineer [the asker] was rash in his judgment. He was extremely unjust to Imām ʿAlī ؑ in his rashness to judge. How could you judge so quickly and say that if you were in Imām ʿAlī's ؑ place, you wouldn't have appointed ʿAbd Allāh b. ʿAbbās? There's nothing to stop us from making speculative judgements about such historical matters. One could judge the deeds of someone who lived five-hundred years ago by saying, "Well, I think if he did this instead of that, it would've been better." There are even those that make definitive judgements. It's wrong to make definitive judgements about anyone, let alone Imām ʿAlī ؑ!

Imām ʿAlī ؑ was living those incidents himself, and he knows ʿAbd Allāh b. ʿAbbās better than you and I do, which also applies to the rest of his companions. And yet we casually come and say if Imām ʿAlī ؑ had chosen anyone other than ʿAbd Allāh b. ʿAbbās, that person would've done a better job, but Imām ʿAlī ؑ failed to do so.

This is rash.

In addition, you constantly say—and we always benefit from your words—that Imām ʿAlī ؑ had a particular policy that he never did, and never should, deviate from. He had no one to aid him and assist him in applying this policy; he was alone. He always spoke of his loneliness and lack of qualified companions.

'Abd Allāh b. 'Abbās, whom you've mentioned, and the rest of them, always came to Imām 'Alī ☙ asking him to be lenient, or as we say these days, diplomatic.

Prove to me that the Imām ☙ had enough competent companions and that he still made mistakes, Allah ☙ forbid. I personally cannot prove that Imām 'Alī ☙ had enough competent companions.

We know that the Prophet ☙ appointed 'Alī ☙ as his successor. Imām 'Alī ☙ spoke out and said that the caliphate was stolen from him, but when they sought him out to pledge allegiance to him after 'Uthmān, he stepped back and said, "Leave me be and seek someone else. We're coming upon something that has many facets and components... The horizon became clouded, and the way became obscured."[175] Imām 'Alī ☙ wanted to say, "Things fell to ruin. I can do nothing and there is no one on my side. I lost my qualified supporters and I no longer have anyone to assist me in reforming society." After this, he says, "If it weren't for the people here and my accountability due to the presence of supporters..." He means that I am now accountable and have no excuse. History will refuse my excuses, and it will say that 'Alī ☙ wasted this opportunity. I know it isn't truly an opportunity, but I will take it because I don't want history to say that it was a good opportunity and I wasted it.

The Imām ☙ himself mentions the lack of qualified individuals and says that the timing was bad. We may doubt any person and hesitate about him, but history itself does not hesitate about Imām 'Alī ☙ who considered himself more entitled to the caliphate than anyone else. The Sunnis themselves say that Imām 'Alī ☙ considered himself more entitled to the caliphate than Abū Bakr and 'Umar.

---

175 Nahj al-Balāgha, sermon 91.

In this case, why did Imām ʿAlī ﷺ hesitate when they rushed to him after the death of ʿUthmān, saying, "I am better for you as a minister than a commander"? We feel from this context that he did not have qualified companions. As for the reasons behind this situation, that's a different question.

Concerning your question about the verse "give the *zakāt* while bowing down"[176] and how rings are not a part of *zakāt*, first of all, any kind of spending for the cause of good is called *zakāt*. The term *zakāt* that is used in juristic custom to refer to the obligatory *zakāt* concerns the conventional *zakāt*. It's not right to say that whenever the Qurʾān mentions those who "maintain the prayer, give the *zakāt*,"[177] it is referring to the obligatory *zakāt*. *Zakāt* is everything that purifies money, and even the spirit and the soul too. The Qurʾān calls any form of financial spending either the *zakāt* of money, the *zakāt* of the spirit, or the *zakāt* of the soul.

The same thing applies to charity (*al-ṣadaqa*). Charity has now become a particular concept, such as giving charity in secret (*ṣadaqat al-sirr*). However, the Qurʾān classifies every good deed as an act of charity. If you built a hospital or wrote a book whose benefit spread in society, this would be an act of charity according to the Qurʾān, an ongoing charity (*ṣadaqa jāriya* specifically

This is why when the scholars of Ahl al-Sunnah want to criticize our understanding of the verse, they do not criticize the usage of the word *zakāt* and say that the *zakāt* does not involve rings. The reason for this is that they are knowledgeable about Arabic and know that the *zakāt* does not concern money alone.

---

[176] Sūrat al-Māʾida, verse 55.

[177] [English translator's note]: Sūrat al-Māʾida, verse 55, Sūrat al-Tawba, verse 71.

The other question is why was the ring given away while bowing in prayer. Past scholars, such as al-Fakhr al-Rāzī, discussed this. He mentioned that Imām ʿAlī ﷺ was so absorbed in prayer that he became unconscious of his own self; at that moment, he would no longer pay attention to anything going on around him. How can it be said that he gave the ring away while praying?

In answering, we say that Imām ʿAlī's ﷺ absorption in prayer is an undoubtable reality. However, this does not mean that all the Friends of Allah are constant. The noble Prophet ﷺ himself had two states. Sometimes, he used to be overcome by the mystical attraction (*jadhba*) to the extent that he couldn't bear the completion of the call to prayer. In such cases, he used to say, "Give us relief, O Bilāl!" It was also mentioned that al-Ḥasan and al-Ḥusayn ﷺ used to climb on his back while he was prostrating. The Prophet ﷺ patiently and calmly waited for them ﷺ to come down without falling, extending his prostration in the process.

Another time, the Prophet ﷺ got up to pray, and someone spat close to his prayer spot. The Prophet ﷺ took a step forward, governed the man's spit with earth using his foot, and went back to his place. The jurists benefited from this incident as they derived rulings related to the prayer from it. Al-Sayyid Baḥr al-ʿUlūm even recited:

As the best of all creation walked with Ibn Ṭāb he opened up a thousand doors.[178]

[178] [English translator's note]: Ibn Ṭāb is a kind of Medinan dates. The verse is a reference to a time when the Prophet ﷺ walked forward mid-prayer with a stalk of dates to rub away some sputum that was in the mosque. See Aghā Buzurg al-Ṭihrānī, *al-Dharīʿa*, 24/114.

The Prophet's ﷺ behavior in this regard has resolved many legal difficulties because it clarified what is permissible and impermissible during prayer, in addition to other things.

This means that spiritual states differ.

There is another explanation that has a mystical basis. Those who believe in mystical taste (*dhawq*) say that when the mystical attraction becomes too complete, it causes a return to this world as well. This means that the person would be absorbed in Allah ﷻ and in His creation. The mystics say this, and I personally accept it although I know many of you in our session do not. I want to say that this state is like being detached from one's own body (*khalʿ al-badan*). Some people who reach this stage become detached for a moment or two, maybe an hour, but other people are perpetually detached. I personally believe in this, and I've seen it with my own eyes. There may be someone sitting with us right now, for example, while experiencing a state of bodily detachment.

From the point of view of the mystics, the state of bodily detachment to the point of not feeling a blade as it is taken out of Imām ʿAlī's ؑ body is actually below the state where he directed himself to the needy person mid-prayer. It's not because Imām ʿAlī ؑ became inattentive to Allah ﷻ and directed himself to the needy person but because his direction toward Allah ﷻ reached such a degree of perfection that he became able to see the world in its entirety. In light of all of these proofs, we cannot denounce the Imām's ؑ donation of his ring mid-prayer.

The Imamate According to the Imāms ﷤

Our topic today is the last part of our discussions about the general features of the Imamate. If we decided to continue the discussion, what we would discuss from now on would be of a textual nature, such as the noble Prophet's ﷺ *ḥadīths* about the Commander of the Believers ﷣ or both their *ḥadīths* about the other Imāms ﷤. We would also mention the *ḥadīths* where every Imām ﷣ talks about his successor.

All of these avenues of discussion have a textual nature that depends on appointment and designation. Some of the elements of our discussion today may be repetitions of things we said earlier, but we will need to go back to them for their connection to the spirit of the Imamate. I will rely on the Imāms' ﷤ *ḥadīths* in "Kitāb al-Hujja" in *al-Kāfī* to read what they had to say about these elements.

I repeatedly pointed out that the Shīʿa's definition of the Imamate, or at least the Imamate according to their Imāms' ﷤ *ḥadīths,* is different from the definition that's widespread among Ahl al-Sunna, and it is different from the issue of government as we understand it today. The Imamate that I am talking about is second only to Prophethood. However, this doesn't mean that the Imamate is below all the ranks of Prophethood. No, I mean that the Imamate is similar to the Prophethood of the great ones among the Prophets ﷤ who also attained the Imamate and combined Prophethood and the Imamate. The Imamate is a spiritual state. When we go back to the *ḥadīths* of the Imāms ﷤ in this regard, we find that they greatly focus on the human being in general, so we must look into the view of man if we want to clarify this idea.

Man: What Kind of Being?

You know that the answer to the question of what kind of being man is derives from two views. According to the first view, man, like all other animals, is a strictly earthly being. This view considers man nothing more than a material being, with the qualification that this material being reached the highest degree of material perfection that matter can reach. Life, based on this view—whether in plants, in animals that are a rank higher, or man who is at the highest rank—is simply a manifestation of the perfection that matter gradually reached throughout the course of its transformations. The conclusion of this view is that only the material element figures in the ontological fabric of this being. The truth is that we refer to this part as an element because we have no other way of expressing it. Any creative and wonderful dimension of this being [such as spiritual activity and spiritual and creative faculties] comes from this material fabric alone.

Based on this logic, the first man in creation should be the lowest version of this being, and then he became more perfect as time went on and he progressed. In this regard, there is no difference between how the ancients viewed the first man, saying he was created directly from the earth, and between the contemporary view that some people believe in. This belief is a theory that deserves contemplation in itself, and it states that at first man was a being that came from lesser beings and underwent transformation that distinguished him from a lesser strain. According to this theory, the origin of the first man goes back to the earth, but he did not literally emerge from the earth as the proponents of the first opinion said.

The First Man in the Qur'ān

When we go back to Islamic and Qur'ānic beliefs, we find that our view of the first man depicts him as more perfect than many people who came after him. He is more perfect than the modern man himself. This is because at the moment that first man came into the realm of existence, he was carrying the responsibility of the vicegerency (*khilāfa*) of Allah ﷻ. To put in another way, that man came already bearing the title of prophethood. In religious logic, this is a point worthy of contemplation. Why did the first man come to Earth a prophet and a proof of Allah ﷻ although the religious view states that prophethood is the fruit of the ordinary trajectory of perfection? This means that the human component should exist first of all and then go on its journey toward elevation and perfection, after which one of its members will be chosen to be a prophet and messenger.

The cause of contemplation is the difference between the latter conception of prophets and prophethood and between the Islamic-Qur'ānic belief that states that the first man came into existence already a Proof and a prophet. The Noble Qur'ān puts the first man in a very lofty position, saying about him: "When your Lord said to the angels, 'Indeed I am going to set a viceroy on the earth,' they said, 'Will You set in it someone who will cause corruption in it, and shed blood, while we celebrate Your praise and proclaim Your sanctity?' He said, 'Indeed I know what you do not know.' And He taught Adam the Names, all of them; then presented them to the angels and said, 'Tell me the names of these."[179]

[179] Sūrat al-Baqara, verse 30-31.

The expression "and breathed into him of My spirit"[180] was mentioned about the first man; it implies the presence of an element from the higher realm within the composition of this being, which is other than material elements. The composition of this being contains something that came from Allah ﷻ, in addition to the attributes of the position of vicegerent that is mentioned in the verse "Indeed I am going to set a viceroy on the earth."[181]

This means that the Qur'ānic vision involves a great detail about man. The first human being to step foot on this earth had the title of the Proof of Allah, the Prophet of Allah ﷺ, and the being connected to heaven and the world of the unseen.

The words of our Imāms ؑ about the Imamate is based on the principle of man's authenticity. This means that the first man in creation had the attributes mentioned earlier, and that the last man in creation will also have those same attributes on this path. Between the first and the last man, the earthly world will never be without a human being of this kind who encapsulates the spirit of "Indeed I am going to set a viceroy on the earth."[182] This is the central point about the issue of the Imamate.

In addition to this fundamental principle, there is the secondary issue that the members of the human race as a whole are an extension of that human being's existence such that if that man did not exist, the rest of the human race could never exist.

---

180 Sūrat al-Ḥijr, verse 29

181 Sūrat al-Baqara, verse 30-31.

182 Sūrat al-Baqara, verse 30-31.

This person is the Proof of Allah, described in *Nahj al-Balāgha*[183] and other books as follows: "I swear by Allah that indeed the earth will never be empty of someone who upholds Allah's proof (*lā takhlū al-arḍ min qāʾimin lil-Lāh bi-ḥujja*)." I heard the late Ayatollah Borujerdi 🕮 say that this sentence is part of some things that Imām ʿAlī 🕮 said in Baṣra; it is recurrent among the Sunnis and the Shīʿa. I can't remember if I came across this information elsewhere or not, and didn't really follow up to find out.

In any case, this sentence came as part of Imām ʿAlī's 🕮 famous talk with Kumayl. Kumayl b. Ziyād says, "The Commander of the Believers ʿAlī b. Abī Ṭālib took me by the hand and led me to graveyard. After he reached the desert, he sighed and said, 'O Kumayl b. Ziyād, hearts are containers, and the best of them are the most aware, so remember what I am saying."

After that, Imām ʿAlī 🕮 divided people into the categorization that he is known for, saying, "People are of three kinds: a divine scholar, a learner on the path to salvation, and the riff raff." It's worth noting here that when the Imām 🕮 speaks of the divine scholar, it is different from when we call someone a scholar out of flattery. The Imām 🕮 is talking about the truly divine scholar who is sincere in his belonging to Allah 🕮. Such a description may only apply to the Prophets 🕮 and the Imāms 🕮. In addition, the mention of the second category—that of the learner—implies that the first category refers to scholars who have not learned their knowledge from other human beings. This would make the learners in the second category the students of the scholars in the first category. As for the riff raff, Imām ʿAlī 🕮 described them as those who "did not see the light of knowledge or take refuge in a sturdy pillar." After that, Imām ʿAlī 🕮 began criticizing the people of his time, saying that he has a lot of

---

[183] *Nahj al-Balāgha*, saying 139

knowledge but cannot find anyone to carry it: "Here lies great knowledge [he pointed to his chest] if only I can find someone to carry it. The Imām ﷺ then says that he indeed came across men with sharp, quick understanding, but they were not trustworthy because they used religion to gain this world.

In addition to this category, Imām ʿAlī ﷺ refers to another one. Although this category appears good for following the carriers of the Truth, it actually has no insight and commits blind imitation without understanding what it is taught or understanding things incorrectly and falling into doubt.[184]

Imām ʿAlī's ﷺ words so far imply that he had almost despaired of finding any carriers of this knowledge, but at the end of his talk with Kumayl, he said,[185] "I swear by Allah that indeed the earth will never be empty of someone who upholds Allah's proof. He is either visible and well-known or afraid and hidden so that the proofs and evidences of Allah do not be invalidated. How many are Allah's proofs and where are they? By Allah, they are the least in number and the greatest in value with Allah. By them, Allah safeguards his proofs and evidences until they entrust them to their peers and implant them in the hearts of their likes. Knowledge charged at them with the reality of insight and they had direct contact with the spirit of certainty. They found easy what the indulgent found hard and they found comfort in what the ignorant found lonesome. They

[184] [Arabic translator's note]: Referring to these two categories, Imām ʿAlī ﷺ says, "But yes. I came across sharp men yet they were not trustworthy. They used religion as a means for this world and used Allah's blessings to vanquish His servants and His proofs to counter His Friends. Otherwise, they submitted to the carriers of the Truth but without insight, the first sign of confusion kindling doubt in their hearts. Away with the latter and former!" See *Nahj al-Balāgha*, saying 147.

[185] [Arabic translator's note]: This is the paragraph that Ayatollah Borujerdi ؒ said that Imām ʿAlī ﷺ uttered in Baṣra. It actually occurs at the end of his talk with Kumayl b. Ziyād.

walked in this world with bodies whose spirits are connected to the higher realm."[186]

Imām ʿAlī ﷺ means that he will not depart from this world without saying what he has to say. In describing those people who receive knowledge from the higher realm of dominion, Imām ʿAlī ﷺ says, "Knowledge charged at them with the reality of insight." This means that knowledge itself is charged at them, not they at it. This indicates that their knowledge comes from emanation (*ifāḍī*) and endows them with true insight without mistake, confusion, or deficit. When Imām ʿAlī ﷺ says, "they had direct contact with the spirit of certainty," this implies that these people have some kind of connection to the higher realm. Things that appear rough and impassable for the indulgent who found comfort in luxury, pleasures, and bliss are easy for them. For example, if it is difficult, or the most difficult of all, for the person who finds comfort in this world and this pleasures to be in solitude with Allah for one hour, those people yearn to this solitude and find comfort in it. They have been described as those who "found comfort in what the ignorant found lonesome."

They are with the people bodily, but their spirits yearn for a loftier horizon and they are connected to the higher realm. When they are seen among the people, the people imagine them to be humans just like them because they do not know about their internal dimension. This is the logic that reflects the spirit and core of the Imamate. In "Kitāb al-Hujja" in *al-Kāfī*, there is a chapter entitled, "If only two

---

[186] *Nahj al-Balāgha*, saying 147.

men remained on earth, one of them would be the Proof."[187] This means that one of them would have these exact characteristics, just like the first man who set foot on this earth.

To better introduce you to this logic, I brought with me "Kitāb al-Hujja" of *al-Kāfī* to read and explain to you passages related to our topic. The main point in this regard is that the rest of the subheadings in this chapter—such as that the Imām should be just or that the people should refer to him in their religious disagreements – are a branch that is dependent on this principle and not the opposite. What I mean is that we don't conclude the necessity of the Imām and the Imamate from people's need for the Imām's rule. This means that the necessity of rulership does not lead to the necessity of the Imām. The Imamate is much more elevated than this.

Based on this logic, issues like rulership and such are benefits dependent on the Imamate. I will choose sentences from every *ḥadīth* to uncover the nature, pillars, and components of this logic.

---

[187] [Arabic translator's note]: This chapter contains five *ḥadīths* that have a similar message and almost identical wording. Some of them are: "If only two people remain on earth, one would be the Proof," "If the earth had only two people on it, the Imām would be one of them," "If humanity were but two people, one of them would be the Imām," and "the Imām is the last person to die so that no one would say to Allah that He left him without a Proof." See "Kitāb al-Hujja" in *al-Kāfī*, 1/179-180.

A Narration from Imām al-Ṣādiq ﷺ

There is a narration related to prophets and messengers ﷺ that came from Imām al-Ṣādiq ﷺ in his answer to the *zindīq*.[188] The *zindīq* asked the Imām, "Where did the prophets and messengers come from?" Imām al-Ṣādiq ﷺ gave him an answer rooted in monotheism: "We proved that we have a Creator and a Maker Who is above us and the rest of His creation. That Maker was wise and transcendent, and it was not fit for Him to be seen by His creation, or touched by them or to engage in direct contact with them that allows them to argue with Him. This proves that He had agents among His creation who spoke on His behalf to His creatures and servants, guiding them to their best interest and advantage and to the things whose performance guaranteed their life and whose abandonment led to their demise. This proves that there are people who command and forbid the creatures of Allah, the Wise and the Knowing, on His behalf."[189]

This text means that there has to be a person who has a special connection to Allah ﷻ that enables him to receive revelation while

---

[188] The word *zindīq* at the time did not have negative connotations that reflect obscenities and foul words like it does in our time. Back then it was the name given to a group, and the members of the group themselves did not consider it obscene or foul. A similar modern-day counterpart would be the term "materialist." Naturally, a monotheist would not like being called a materialist, but for the materialist himself that is a source of pride. Much has been said about the word *zindīq*. The most reliable of these sayings is that the *zanādiqa* were Manicheans who emerged at the beginning of the second Hijri century, which is the century when Imām al-Ṣādiq ﷺ was alive. Many European and other thinkers looked into the roots of *zandaqa* in Islam, and their most important conclusion that it was an expression of Manicheanism. Mānī's religion was against Allah ﷻ, as Mānī alleged that he was a prophet. However, Mānī was not a monotheist but a dualist. Mānī was even more of a dualist than Zoroaster. Many even thought it probable that Zoroaster was a monotheist or at least someone who believed in oneness of Allah's ﷻ essence (*al-tawḥīd al-dhātī*), but his words do not imply creational oneness (*tawḥīd al-khāliqiyya*). In any case, he believed in a source without beginning that created the world. Mānī, on the other hand, was definitely a dualist who considered himself a prophet of the god of goodness. The Manicheans who came after Mānī had a tendency toward materialism, and eventually they stopped believing in anything at all.

[189] [Arabic translator's note]: See "Kitāb al-Hujja: The Need for al-Ḥujja" in *al-Kāfī*, 1/168.

also having contact with us. The existence of such a person is necessary, like we already said. Imām al-Ṣādiq ﷺ continues: "They are wise people who have been disciplined through wisdom and sent with it. They are unlike the people despite being like them in being created." Although they are similar to other people in creation and composition, they ought to be different from them in some respects because they have a higher dimension and a higher spirit. Elsewhere, Imām al-Ṣādiq ﷺ says about these individuals, "The Wise and Knowledgeable [Allah] aided them with wisdom," and states that they must exist at every time: "that has been the case in every era and time." Why is that? "So that Allah's earth would not be void of a Proof that points to the truth of His words and justice."[190]

Zayd b. ʿAlī and the Issue of the Imamate

Zayd b. ʿAlī b. al-Ḥusayn, the brother of Imām al-Bāqir ﷺ, is an esteemed and righteous man. Our Imāms ﷺ spoke highly of him and praised his revolt. There is a disagreement about Zayd, which revolves around the question of whether he was seeking revolt for his own sake or for commanding the right and forbidding the wrong and returning the caliphate to his brother al-Bāqir ﷺ. The fact that may be agreed on is that our Imāms ﷺ spoke highly of him and called him a martyr. In *al-Kāfī* itself, we read that the Imāms ﷺ said about him, "By Allah, he passed away a martyr."

An issue still remains, whose significance is this: was Zayd in error or not? The narration that I will mention now shows that he was in error. However, the question of how such a person may be in error does not concern us here.

[190] [Arabic translator's note]: Ibid.

Imām al-Bāqir ﷺ had a companion known as Abū Ja'far al-Aḥwal. Abū Ja'far narrates that Zayd was in hiding and sent after him. When Abū Ja'far came to him, Zayd asked, "O Abū Ja'far, what would you say if one of us came to you, would you support him?" Abū Ja'far said, "I said to him, 'If it was your father or brother, I would." Zayd asked Abū Ja'far to support him and said, "I want to go and wage *jihād* against these people. Support me." Abū Ja'far refused and said, "May I be made ransom for you, but I will not do so." Zayd asked, "You refuse to support me?" Abū Ja'far responded, "I said to him, "I only have one soul. If Allah has a Proof on His earth, those who stay behind are saved and those who go out with you are doomed. If Allah did not have a Proof on His earth, those who stay behind and those who go out with you are alike."

Abū Ja'far realized Zayd's intention; that's why he told him that Allah ﷻ has a Proof on His earth. His meaning was that the Proof of this age is your brother, not you. At this point, Zayd started telling Abū Ja'far that his father Imām al-Bāqir ﷺ loves him dearly, so why has he never told him about this? Abū Ja'far says that Zayd told him, "O Abū Ja'far, when I used to sit with my father at the table, he used to feed me bites rich with clarified butter by his own hand and blow on hot bites for me until they cooled out of pity for me. Are you saying he didn't pity me for the Fire of Hell that he told you the religion without telling me?" Abū Ja'far replied, "May I be made ransom for you. It's precisely because he pitied you the Fires of Hell that he didn't tell you. He was worried that you would not accept what he had to say and end up in the Fire for it. He told me because if I accepted what he had to say, I would be saved, and if I did not accept it, it didn't matter to him if I went to the Fire." Abū Ja'far mentions that he asked Zayd, "Are you better or are the prophets better?" Zayd said, "The prophets are better." Abū Ja'far said, "Ya'qūb told Yūsuf, 'My son, do not recount your dream to your brothers, lest they should devise schemes against you' [Sūrat Yūsuf, verse 5]. Yaʿqūb was a prophet, and Yūsuf was a prophet and the successor of his father. Despite this, Yaʿqūb forbade Yūsuf from recounting his dream to his brothers. This prohibition was not out of hatred but out of love." Abū Jaʿfar continued, "Why didn't Yaʿqūb warn his sons so that they wouldn't devise schemes against Yūsuf? He chose to keep it a secret from them. Your father is the same: he kept it a secret from you because he feared for you."

When the conversation got to that point, Zayd was at a dead end and did not know what to say. He finally added, "Now that you've said that, your man in Medina [meaning Zayd's brother Imām al-Bāqir] told me that I will be killed and crucified at al-Kunāsa, and that he has a scroll mentioning this." Zayd here seems like he had a total change of heart; his logic now supported the second point of view. At the beginning, he dismissed the idea and he seemed to be actively ignoring it at the beginning of his talk with Abū Jaʿfar. After he saw Abū Jaʿfar's steadfastness about the Imamate, however, he told him that he also believes in this dimension of the Imamate and is not ignorant of it. His final sentence to Abū Jaʿfar indicates that was deliberately determined on rebelling in accordance with the directions of his brother Imām al-Bāqir. Abū Jaʿfar said that when he went to perform the pilgrimage, he told Imām al-Ṣādiq about his conversation with Zayd and he supported his views and conclusions.[191]

---

[191] [Arabic translator's note]: Imām al-Ṣādiq ﷺ said to Abū Jaʿfar when he told him about his conversation with Zayd, "You stumped him and left him with nowhere to go with his excuses." See See "Kitāb al-Hujja: The Need for al-Ḥujja" in *al-Kāfī, ḥadīth* number 5, 1/174

Two *Ḥadīths* From Imām al-Ṣādiq

In a *ḥadīth*, Imām al-Ṣādiq says, "The earth will never be without an Imām," and "If two people were left on earth, one would be the Proof over the other."[192]

A Narration from Imām al-Riḍā

There are many *ḥadīths* in this regard, including a detailed narration from Imām al-Riḍā from ʿAbd al-ʿAzīz b. Muslim. ʿAbd al-ʿAzīz b. Muslim says, "We were with al-Riḍā in Marv and we gathered in the mosque on Friday when we first arrived. Someone mentioned the Imamate and said that the people are heavily divided about it. I went to my master al-Riḍā and told him what the people were saying; he smiled." The smile here was out of ridicule of those people and their ignorance about the Imamate. ʿAbd al-ʿAzīz continues, "The Imām said, 'O ʿAbd al-ʿAzīz, the people are ignorant and they have been deceived. Allah did not call His Prophet to Him until he perfected the religion for him and revealed to him the Qurʾān that contains the explanation of everything. In the Qurʾān, Allah clarified the permissible and the prohibited and the punishments and rulings, in addition to everything that people need without deficit. Allah says, "We have not omitted anything from the Book.' During the farewell pilgrimage toward the end of the Prophet's life, Allah revealed "Today I have perfected your religion for you, and I have completed My blessing upon you, and I have approved Islam as your religion."[193] The Imamate is part of religion's completion. The Prophet did not pass without explaining to his *ummah* the features of its religion and showing it the way. He

---

[192] [Arabic translator's note]: For the first *ḥadīth* see *al-Kāfī*, *ḥadīth* number 2, 1/178, for the second *ḥadīth*, see ibid., *ḥadīth* number 2, 1/179.

[193] Sūrat al-Māʾida, verse 3.

left them hoping that they will walk the path of the Truth and established ʿAlī as a guidepost and an Imām for them."

The logic of the Qurʾān explicitly states that it contains an explanation for everything. The question that arises is this: did the Book of Allah explain the particularities and details as well or did it limit the explanations to generalities and universal principles that people need?

One of the details that the Qurʾān explains is that it appointed an authority that the people could refer to after the Prophet ﷺ to interpret and explain the Qurʾān and clarify its universal principles and their details. This figure of authority does not do this of his own volition or based on his own opinions, sometimes being correct and other times making mistakes in his *ijtihād*. This figure does his duty through divine knowledge, and he possesses the truth of Islam. This clarifies the meaning of the Qurʾān's explanation of everything. It explained principles and generalities and gave the knowledge of the details and particularities to the appointed authority who lives among the people and who knows everything about Islam.

This leaves nothing unexplained. The Qurʾān contains the generalities and it gave the details to the authority/ Imām. This is what is meant when we say that the Qurʾān explained everything. Let's go back to the narration. Imām al-Riḍā ﵇ continues: "Do they know the value and position of the Imamate that their choices about it are valid?" They believe in the election of the Imām because they think that electing an Imām is like electing an army commander for example although the Qurʾān stated that religion was perfected with the appointment of the Imām who knows the truth of Islam and the particularities that weren't mentioned in the Qurʾān. Can the people know such a person to elect him? Talking about electing the Imām is like talking about electing the Prophet ﷺ!

Imām al-Riḍā ﷺ adds: "The Imamate is far greater, more inviolable, and deeper than anything that the people's intellects can reach or have opinions about, electing an Imām by their own choice." This text states that the Imamate transcends the thoughts of the people and cannot be an electoral issue that is based on their own choice. A popular, electoral issue is any issue that can really be decided by society. Religion does not directly interfere in issues that the people may determine by themselves. In such a case, it's even wrong for religion to interfere. Otherwise, what's the use of man's intellect and thought if he does not engage them in this domain? This domain is an open space for man's intellect and thought, and through it people can practice their right to choose. However, when the issue is out of the bounds of human intellect, this leaves no room for choice. The issue of the Imamate is like this, as the Imām is "far greater, more inviolable, and deeper" than being understood through people's intellects, opinions, and choices.

If you want to understand the true meaning of the Imamate, know that it is different from what people think it is in our age, i.e. it is the election of the Prophet's ﷺ successor who should only manage the affairs of the *ummah*. According to Imām al-Riḍā ﷺ, "Allah accorded the Imamate to His friend Ibrāhīm after giving him prophethood and friendship. Joyful, Ibrāhīm asked, 'And from among my descendants?'[194] although he knew that this position cannot include all his descendants. He received the answer, 'My pledge does not extend to the unjust.'"[195] The question arises about the identity of the unjust. Is someone unjust when they commit

---

[194] Sūrat al-Baqara, verse 124.

[195] Sūrat al-Baqara, verse 124.

injustice, whether they were unjust in the past or not? It has been mentioned that it's impossible for Ibrāhīm ﷺ to ask this position for his unjust descendants. This means that he was asking it for the righteous among them. The answer that he ﷺ received was that the Imamate will be the lot of the righteous to the exclusion of the unjust. Imām al-Riḍā ﷺ says, "This verse invalidated the Imamate of every unjust person until the Day of Judgment and limited the Imamate to the elect." The elect (*ṣafwa*) are the best of their kind. To go back to Imām al-Riḍā ﷺ: "Allah honored Ibrāhīm by establishing the Imamate in the elect and pure of his descendants, saying, 'And We gave him Isaac, and Jacob as well for a grandson, and each of them We made righteous. We made them imams, guiding by Our command, and We revealed to them the performance of good deeds.'"[196] The word pure here indicates infallibility.

The Qur'ān gave great importance to giving Ibrāhīm's descendants the Imamate, which gave great reinforcement to the issue of the Imamate. The question that arises here is why did the Qur'ān focus so much on this dimension although it refuses genealogical favoritism and racism? Muḥammad Taqī Sharī'atī explained this remarkably well in his *Khilāfat va-vilāyat.* He differentiated between a genealogy as an ancestral and a natural entity and between a genealogy's qualifications. These qualifications make all the difference and they are the reason that the Imamate was given to specific descendants.

Imām al-Riḍā ﷺ then says, "How can these ignorant ones choose?" He's asking how these people may elect the Imām although the Imamate is the position given to Ibrāhīm ﷺ only after he attained prophethood. The Imamate is an inheritance among trustees, which

---

[196] Sūrat al-Anbiyā', verses 72-73.

makes it an aptitude that gets transferred from one generation to another, and not a legal kind of inheritance. It is the first man's vicegerency of Allah ﷻ and the succession of the Prophet ﷺ. Given these characteristics, can it depend on the choice and election of the people? Imām al-Riḍā ؑ says, "The Imamate is the position of the prophets and the inheritance of the trustees. The Imamate is the vicegerency of Allah and the succession of the Prophet ... The Imamate is the preserver of religion, the order of the Muslims, the righteousness of this world, and the might of the faithful. The Imamate is Islam's growing root and its elevated branch. Through the Imām, prayer, the zakāt, fasting, the pilgrimage, and jihād find their completion."197

Conclusion

All that's been said leads to a certain logic. If we accept this logic, it has principles and components, and if someone rejects it, that requires further discussion. The components of this logic are different from unimportant, superficial matters such as the questions of most theologians. They say that Abū Bakr became the first caliph after the death of the Prophet ﷺ while ʿAlī ؑ was the fourth. They ask whether ʿAlī ؑ should've actually been the first or the fourth and whether Abū Bakr fulfilled the conditions of the Imamate. This kind of discussion details the conditions and characteristics of the Imamate, which are also the conditions of the rule and ruler of the Muslims.

Naturally, the conditions of rulership and the characteristics of the ruler are important, and the Shīʿa have apt objections and criticisms. However, it is essentially incorrect to reduce the issue of the Imamate to the question of whether Abū Bakr fulfilled the

---

197 [Arabic translator's note]: For the full text, see "Kitāb al-Hujja" in *al-Kāfī*, 1/198-203.

conditions of the Imamate. Ahl al-Sunnah do not believe in such a position. They say that Allah ﷻ revealed the unseen supernatural dimensions of man to Ādam, Ibrāhīm, and the rest of the Prophets until the circle was closed with the Prophet ﷺ. As for the time after the Prophet ﷺ, it only had ordinary human beings without exceptional people like the Imām. There were only scholars who gained their knowledge through learning and striving, and who may be correct or incorrect. There were also righteous and profligate rulers.

In light of that, the Sunni conception of the post-Prophetic era does not include believing, like we do, in Proofs of Allah who are connected to the supernatural world. They believe that this door was firmly closed with the death of the Prophet ﷺ. What we Shīʿa say is that the message and prophethood were concluded after the Prophet ﷺ such that no other human being will ever bring humanity a new law and religion. There is only one religion, and it is Islam. With the Prophet ﷺ of Islam, the message and prophethood were concluded. The line of the Proof and Perfect Man, however, has never been cut off in humanity. The first human being was a Perfect Man, and so should be the last. There is one group of Sunnis that does accept this logic, and they are the Sufis, but they express it in other terms. This explains why Sunni Sufis accept the Shīʿa's views in this regard.

Take al-Andalus for example. It was a land whose people were not only Sunnis; they actively opposed the Shīʿa in a way that implied *naṣb*. This is because the Umayyads were the first to conquer those lands and subjected them to their rule; the Umayyads opposed Ahl al-Bayt. This is why some of the *nāṣibī* Sunni scholars are Andalusian. Perhaps there were no Shīʿa at all in al-Andalus, and if there were any, they must've been a few.

Despite this, and although Muḥyī al-Dīn b. ʿArabī was an Andalusian, he believed that the earth can never be without a guardian and a Proof. He advocates the Shīʿī belief in this regard and mentions the Imāms 🕊️ by name until the twelfth Imām 🕊️. He mentions that he saw the Imām Muḥammad b. al-Ḥasan al-ʿAskarī 🕊️ somewhere a few years after 600 AH. This belief goes back to Ibn ʿArabī's mystical inclinations.

Of course, Ibn ʿArabī has words that contradict this and indicate that he was a zealous Sunni. However, his mystical taste necessitates the belief that the earth will never be without what they call a guardian and our Imāms 🕊️ call a Proof. He goes beyond that belief to say that he actually saw this guardian and met Muḥammad b. al-Ḥasan al-ʿAskarī 🕊️, visiting him in the place he is hidden. The Imām 🕊️ was then three hundred and some years old.

Audience Q and A

Question: The disagreement between the Shīʿa and the Sunnis is about guardianship and the caliphate. Many Shīʿa who do not truly know the position of the Imamate unfortunately fell into error and doubtfully asked how the Qurʾān could mention the word guardianship but not the word caliphate, although the two are different? This error led me on a search to see if *mawlā* has the same meaning as caliph. In my search, I found in the Arabic dictionary that one of the meanings of *mawlā* is *khalīf*. I believe this finding removes the confusion. What I want to ask is this: is the correct Arabic term *khalīfa* or *khalīf*? The Qurʾān of course only mentions the *khalīfa*.

Answer: It's not like you said. The term *khalīfa* in the Qurʾān does not occur in this meaning [the political-social leadership of the caliphs after the Prophet ﷺ. However, the term does occur frequently in the narrations of the Shīʿa. The word *khalīfa* …

Asker: I mean the *khalīfa* of Allah.

Answer: The *khalīfa* of Allah is one thing and the *khalīfa* of the Prophet ﷺ is another. A *khalīfa* is someone who acts as deputy on someone's behalf and takes it upon himself to do that other person's duties. We should not focus too much on whether this term occurred in the Qurʾān or Sunnah or not. The most important thing is the mention of the meaning, regardless of whether the actual term is mentioned or not. As for what you kindly mentioned about *mawlā* meaning *khalīf*, that is not correct. I think you might've gotten confused. The dictionary mentions the word *ḥalīf* and not *khalīf*.

A *ḥalīf* is someone who goes into alliance with other people. The word *mawlā* also means supporter. The Arabs sometimes had alliances, and the tribes would enter into alliances and be called allies (*ḥulafāʾ*). The word *ḥalīf* is given to people on both sides of an alliance. Even if they were only two people, one would be the ally and supporter of the other. If the word *mawlā* came with the meaning of *ḥalīf*, it would also mean supporter.

Appendix[198]

The Imamate: Safeguarding the Religion

Muslim theologians have had a lot to say about the Imām's duty of safeguarding the religion. They often expressed this duty with an example that goes like this. If we suppose that a building was built, it would be necessary to protect it from time and the elements such as damage from wind or rain and the like. In countering this example, they said that a building erected by incomparably great builders does not need guardians at that same level of greatness. For examples, buildings like Sheikh Lotfollah Mosque, Shah Mosque, Ali Qapu Palace, and the geometric patterns (*zakhārif*) of Goharshad Mosque, as well as the calligraphy in hand-written Qur'āns do not require guardians that are as great as their creators.

However, the truth is that error in religion does not happen so simply; it has a different trajectory. For psychological and social reasons, any uprising and revolution stops targeting the enemy as soon as it achieves success and becomes certain of the enemy's despair of achieving victory. Slowly, the enemy itself joins the ranks of the uprising without actually believing in it. It does so out of self-interest and personal advantage. This aptly describes the opposers of the Constitutional Revolution in Iran. The enemies of this revolution joined it and pretended to eagerly support it such that some of them actually became prime ministers.

After joining the revolution, these figures preserved its exterior and even gave it greater magnificence while robbing it of its spirit and essence. They hollowed the revolution of its meaning and truth and

198 [Arabic translator's note]: This appendix comprises the notes that were found in the margins of the books Shahīd Muṭahharī used to read and in his notebooks and papers. The publisher included the notes that are relevant to the Imamate at the beginning of the book, but I thought it better to insert them as an appendix after translating four into Arabic and omitting the fifth because it is not very relevant.

made it an empty husk that has no core. Imām ʿAlī ﷺ expressed this state by saying, "Islam will be poured out like the contents of a container are poured out." This leads to steering the uprising away from its course and reversing its meaning while keeping its form. People would be more than happy by this because the vast majority of them are content with external appearances. Even more, they would be thankful because the slogans that they hold dear are given the highest regard. No matter that the foundations have been eroded!

What's required in such a case is maturity and far-reaching insight. This means that the report "In every generation, we have counterparts that drive away the distortion of the extremists and the impersonation of the falsifiers" may either be a reference to the pure Imāms ﷺ themselves or to righteous scholars who watch over people's beliefs after the Imāms ﷺ. Standing up to innovations is not limited to the familiar kind of innovations, i.e. inserting new things into religion, such as creating new *sunnahs* and laws and explicitly attributing them to religion. These innovations might get to a point where society would denounce authentic religious thought.

I want to emphasize that we shouldn't worry about external influences over Islam but about internal influences. The Qurʾān itself stated, "Today the faithless have despaired of your religion. So do not fear them, but fear Me."[199] The internal threats to Islam are not limited to the corruption and debauchery (*fujūr*) that are caused by desires and other reasons. These threats extend to internal hypocrisy and the forces that are afraid of confronting Islam head-on. What they do is wear the mask of Islam to establish their questionable goals. They disfigure Islam and hollow it from the

[199] Sūrat al-Māʾida, verse 3.

inside out by focusing on Islamic slogans. This way, they destroy the meaning and preserve the husks. This enables them to alter the course and goal by practicing moral distortion (see the notes on distortion).[200] We should fear these people and the possibility that naive Muslims who may be tricked by this group of hypocrites who falsely pretend to practice Islam.

The Imamate/Leadership

The papers entitled "Notes on Leadership and Management" contain a useful standard to distinguish between prophethood and the Imamate. The former means guidance (i.e. showing the way) while the latter means leading (i.e. taking people by the hand and getting them to their destination). Just as religious guidance should come from the realm of the unseen and the guide should be appointed by the realm of the unseen, the same applies to leadership. The noble Prophet ﷺ and some other Prophets عليهم السلام were guides and leaders at the same time (i.e. both prophets and Imāms). With the final prophethood, divine guidance with the meaning of showing the way ended, but divine leadership with the meaning of getting others to their destination still continues. Those papers also mention that the Imamate and prophethood are positions that may be separated sometimes. Many messengers were also prophets who communicated the revelation without being Imāms. Our Imāms عليهم السلام are also only Imāms without being prophets. There is a third possibility that concerns Muḥammad and Ibrāhīm عليهما السلام who were

---

[200] [Arabic translator's note]: When I went back to these notes, I found the following words by the author: "Moral distortion is interpreting words in a different way to serve one's goals while outwardly using the same words. This is like Muʿāwiya's interpretation of the text concerning ʿAmmār b. Yāsir: 'You will be killed by the transgressing group (al-fiʾa al-bāghiya).' This is moral distortion. Another example is the Khawārij's use of the verse 'Sovereignty (al-ḥukm) belongs only to Allah' (Sūrat Yūsuf, verse 40) in order to raise the slogan 'Arbitration (al-ḥukm) is only Allah's.' Imām ʿAlī's ؏ response was: 'A word of truth whose intention is falsehood.' This also is distortion and misinterpretation of the verse. It was done either intentionally or out of ignorance and has led Islam into a world of trouble. Another example of moral distortion is the ḥadīth: 'If you have knowledge, do whatever you like.'"

both prophets and Imāms. Allah ﷻ said [to Ibrāhīm]: "I am making you the Imam of mankind."[201] The duty of the Imām is to be the leader, manager, and leader of those who accept his leadership and Imamate.

The Shīʿa believe that just as prophethood (religious guidance) comes from Allah ﷻ, so does leadership (the Imamate). In this regard, they do not differentiate between guidance and leadership, as both come from Allah ﷻ. The great ones among the prophets [*ulū al-ʿazm*] were guides and leaders at the same time [prophets and Imāms]. The final prophethood ended divine guidance and showing the way, but the ending of this guidance that is prophethood does not mean ending the path of divine leadership, i.e. the Imamate. *Al-Madkhal ilā al-qiyāda* distinguishes between guidance and leadership on page 76 by saying, "From a certain angle, the leader is the person who leads the group to the causes that facilitate reaching its goals. In other words, the leader [Imām] is the one who facilitates achieving purposes and the guide who takes people by the hand. His duty is sometimes not limited to showing the way, as he may supply the tools for walking the way and reaching its end."

In truth, there is partial overlap, depending on the case, between guidance and leadership. Like I said, prophethood is a kind of guidance and the Imamate is a kind of leadership. There is a partial overlap between these two positions. A person may only be a guide without being a promulgator like all of our preachers who promulgate the message properly. This does not include preachers with incorrect teachings of course. A promulgator stands to one side and shows people the way and its pitfalls, leaving them free to follow it or refuse it. In contrast, a person may be a leader but not a

---

[201] Sūrat al-Baqara, verse 124.

guide. In this case, the right way is already established and the goal is clear. The achievement of the goal only requires forces that focus capabilities, organize them, and rearrange them, awakening passive energies and mobilizing them to build and create. Lastly, both duties may be combined in one person, making him a guide and leader at the same time.

The Imamate of the Pure Imāms: Ḥadīth al-Thaqalayn

This is a recurrent *ḥadīth* among the Sunnis and the Shīʿa: "I am leaving among you the notable two, the Book of Allah and my family." In this regard, one may consult Shaykh Qavām Vishnoi's treatise that came out as an appendix to the journal *Risālat al-Islām* as well as the volume [multiple volumes in the newer editions] on the biography and directions of the Prophet ﷺ in *Biḥār al-anwār.*

The preachers of ʿAshūrāʾ usually take this *ḥadīth* as a starting point to speaking about the calamity of Imām al-Ḥusayn ؑ and the neglect of the family that the Prophet ﷺ entrusted to the *ummah* while the soil of his grave was still fresh. This created the impression that the family of the Prophet ؑ had no role and influence. This is incorrect. It is true that Islamic society has not benefited from the Prophet's family ؑ to the utmost, but this family still had an exceptional effect on safeguarding the legacy of Islam.

Obviously, the caliphate, the form of government, and Islamic political life all suffered deviation away from the authentic path, and the family of the Prophet ؑ was unable to do its role in this regard. However, it still preserved the moral and spiritual aspects of Islam and the spiritual inheritance of the Prophet ﷺ, keeping them alive. The Islamic caliphate itself gradually faded away but the spiritual inheritances of Islam remained intact.

Islam is a comprehensive religion that encompasses the external and spiritual dimensions of human life. It is not like schools of thought that rely on a specific teacher or philosopher whose activity is limited to some books and a few students that he brings out to the social arena. Islam practically founded a new system and an original way of thinking, establishing new structures and frameworks. Precisely because Islam is a moral, pedagogical, and educational movement, it is also a social and political order. In its methodology, Islam preserved meaning through substance, the internal dimension though the external dimension, the Hereafter though this world, the core through the husks, and the seed through the fruit.

However, the straying of the caliphate from its authentic path and the deviation of governance from its established methodology turned the system of the caliphate into an empty husk that has no core. Certain titles remained, such as "the Commander of the Believers" and "the successor of the Prophet of Allah," and rulership remained connected to Allah ﷻ and the Prophet ﷺ. However, Islamic life lost all meaning; piety, honesty, justice, beneficence (*iḥsān*), love, equality, and knowledge were nowhere to be found. This was particularly true in the Umayyad era that waged a war against Islamic knowledge and sought to promote pre-Islamic poetry, customs, and traditions, and established the spirit of taking pride in one's ancestors and lineage.

At that moment precisely, politics became practically separated from religion. Those who held and safeguarded the spiritual inheritance of Islam moved away from politics and couldn't interfere. As for those who were in charge of leadership and Islamic politics, they were estranged from the moral spirit of Islam. They only engaged in some formal practices such as Friday and communal prayers and attaining titles. At the end, even these formal appearances were abandoned and the rule went back to its pre-Islamic form, and scholars and religion were totally disconnected from politics.

At the time of Abū Bakr and ʿUmar, politics and religion were still intertwined. However, their reigns planted the first seeds of the separation between the two. ʿUmar constantly made mistakes and ʿAlī corrected him. The mistakes were so frequent that ʿAlī became the person ʿUmar always went back to. This was the great danger threatening the Islamic world. This is why the biggest aspiration of those who wanted the elevation of Islam was the joining of politics and religion again. The relation between the two is like the relation between the body and the spirit. The spirit and the body and the husks and the core have to be connected. The purpose of the husks is that they protect the core. The husks derive their purpose from the core, keeping it safe and protecting it.

Islam's focus on politics, government, *jihād*, and political systems aims to protect the spiritual inheritances and safeguard monotheism, spiritual and moral knowledge, social justice, equality, and basic humanity. If the husks are separated from the core, the core will be subject to harm. If the core is harmed, the husks will be pointless and their fate will be burning and neglect.

The pure Imāms' spirit moved them to safeguard Islam and its spiritual inheritances. For this reason, they distinguished between the system of the caliphate and Islam. The first person who made this distinction was Imām al-Ḥusayn; his uprising proved that Islam is an expression of the values of piety, monotheism, and sacrifice on the way of Allah. Imām al-Ḥusayn showed that

Islam is not the same as the things that the Umayyad caliphate based itself upon. Now, let's look into the nature of the spiritual inheritances of Islam and how the pure Imāms protected them.

Allah says, "to recite to them His signs, to purify them, and to teach them the Book and wisdom,"[202] "so that mankind may maintain justice,"[203] and "Indeed We have sent you as a witness, as a bearer of good news and as a warner and as a summoner to Allah by His permission."[204] First, the Imāms commanded the right and forbade the wrong. The Ḥusaynī uprising was the clearest manifestation of upholding this obligation. Second, the Imāms took it upon themselves to spread knowledge. An example is the school of Imām al-Ṣādiq; Imām al-Ṣādiq gave Islam students such as Hishām b. al-Ḥakam, Zurāra b. Aʿyan, and Jābir b. Ḥayyān. Another way of spreading knowledge was the presence of *Nahj al-Balāgha* and *al-Ṣaḥīfa al-Sajjādiyya* as well as the Imāms' discussions and debates, particularly those of Imām al-Riḍā.

In addition, the Imāms had practical piety, abstinence, selflessness, and beneficence toward Allah's creation. They were known for staying up all night to worship, taking care of the weak and the poor, and having high morals such as forgiveness, generosity, and humility. Their vision was a reminder of the spirituality of Islam and the morals of the Prophet. Mūsā b. Jaʿfar spent entire nights absorbed in worship right by the palace of al-Rashīd. Precisely when he was the heir apparent [of al-Maʾmūn], Imām al-Riḍā was calling out: "There is one Lord and one father and mother [Adam and Eve]; the only merit is piety." He committed

---

[202] Sūrat Jumuʿa, verse 2.

[203] Sūrat al-Ḥadīd, verse 25.

[204] Sūrat al-Aḥzāb, verse 46.

to his words, eating with the doormen and talking kindly to the attendants. The existence of religious knowledge is based on safeguarding the spiritual inheritances of Islam and protecting the core instead of the husks. Separating the knowledgeable scholars from politics was like separating the core from the husks.

The meanings of this *ḥadīth* are recurrent. In addition to its recurrence in meaning, this *ḥadīth* occurred in most narrations with the following wording: "I am leaving among you the notable two, the Book of Allah and my family. As long as you hold on to them, you will never go astray. The two will never be separated until they return to me at my Pool."

In the second issue of its fourth volume, the journal *Risālat al-Islām*, by Dār al-Taqrīb in Cairo, published an article. The author of this article cited the *ḥadīth* like this: "I am leaving among you the notable two, the Book of Allah and my *sunnah*." This caused the late Ayatollah Borujerdi ﵀ to ask one virtuous student in Qum, Shaykh Qavām Vishnoi, to prepare a treatise on the sources of the *ḥadīth*. The treatise was entitled "Ḥadīth al-Thaqalayn," and it was sent to Dār al-Taqrīb. The publishing house issued it as an independent publication. The author of the treatise traced the sources of the *ḥadīth* in the books of the Sunnis and tracked it down in exegetical, *sīra*, historical, and linguistic books. He tracked it down in exegetical works for example by looking at the exegesis of the verse "We shall soon make Ourselves unoccupied for you, O you notable two!"[205] and the verses on holding fast, loving the Prophet's relatives, and purification.[206] In language books, Shaykh Vishnoi traced the *ḥadīth* by looking into the root *th.q.l* for example. Shaykh

[205] Sūrat al-Raḥmān, verse 31.

[206] [English translator's note]: Sūrat al-Āl ʿImrān, verse 103, Sūrat al-Shūrā, verse 23, and Sūrat al-Aḥzāb, verse 33.

Vishnoi said that the *ḥadīth* occurred in *Ṣaḥīḥ Muslim*, 7/122, *Sunan al-Tirmidhī*, 2/307, *al-Sunan al-Dāwūdiyya*, 2/432, *Musnad Aḥmad*, 3/14, 17, 26, 59 and 4/366, 371, 5/182, 189, *Mustadrak al-Ḥākim*, 3/109, *al-Ṭabaqāt*, 4/8, *Usd al-ghāba*, 2/12, 3/147 and in the explanation of the term *ʿitra* in *Sharḥ Nahj al-Balāgha*.

The Qur'ān used the term *al-thaqalān* to refer to humans and the *jinn*. What we should look into is why this particular term was used in the *ḥadīth*. There are several points that require research. First, why were Ahl al-Bayt called a *thiql*? Second, why was the Qur'ān described as the greater *thiql* and Ahl al-Bayt described as the lesser *thiql*? Some narrations are worded to say that one *thiql* is greater than the other.[207] In other reports, the Prophet is asked, "What are *al-thaqalān*?" He says, "The Book of Allah, one end of which is in the hand of Allah and the other is in your hands, and the lesser *thiql*, my family." Some reports include the sentence: "They are two cords that cannot be severed until the Day of Judgment."

The third point is the fact that the noble Prophet said, "The two will never be separated." This does not mean that they will never be separated due to disagreement, war, and argument [as that can never happen in the first place]. The meaning is that holding on to them cannot be piecemeal. There are some who want to separate the two under the pretext of "The Book of Allah is enough for us," like ʿUmar said in the formative period of Islam. Another example is the statement: "The sayings of Ahl al-Bayt are enough for us" that some Akhbārī Shīʿīs abide by, and that is applied in practice by most of the scholars of the Shīʿa. However, such a separation

---

[207] [Arabic translator's note]: In his chain of transmission from Zayd b. al-Arqam, al-Tirmidhī narrated the *ḥadīth* in the following way: "The Prophet of Allah said, 'I am leaving among you that which if you hold fast to, you will not go astray after me. One is greater than the other: the Book of Allah, a cord extended from heaven to earth, and my family who are the people of my household. The two will not be separated until they return to me at my Pool. Consider how you will treat them after me.'" See al-Tirmidhī, *Sunan*, 5/328, *ḥadīth* 3876.

cannot be. The fourth point is the guarantee given by the Prophet ﷺ that if people hold fast to these notable two, they will never go astray.

The components of the Muslims' degradation and deviation began precisely at the point when some people wanted to separate the two. Now we ought to look into the reason it is impossible to separate the Book of Allah and the family of the Prophet ﷺ. The question that arises is this: Why do the Sharia and the divine Book require an additional element by their side? This is related to the depth of the Qur'ān and the need of the *Sharia* for an interpreter. To give an example that better explains things, we import simple things like textiles, shoes, and food containers. In this case, we do not need an expert to accompany these imports. We can simply benefit from the textiles right after we sew them and take advantage of the shoes and food containers directly without need for an expert. However, if we import a factory, we need a specialist and expert to accompany it, set it up, and supervise its management for a period of time until local expertise becomes familiar with it. The same thing applies to importing advanced weaponry. Technicians should accompany it and spend years teaching and training local experts. As an example, we heard that France has sold Libya Mirage aircrafts, but that the Libyan pilots will not be able to operate these aircrafts for at least two years.

The Imamate means Islamic religious authority. This is what the noble Prophet was referring to in this recurrent *ḥadīth*. Religious authority, i.e. the Imām, is the side that undertakes interpreting the Qur'ān, explaining its purposes and rulings, and clarifying the kinds of knowledge and morals included in it. In this regard, simple customary understanding is not enough, so it cannot be said that everyone who knows Arabic understands the Qur'ān. We've seen the deviations caused by this calculated absence [of religious authority/the Imamate]. An example of these deviations is believing in anthropomorphism (*tajsīm*) by saying that you will see your Lord on the Day of Judgment as clearly as you can see the full moon. The claim "The Book of Allah is enough for us" could only produce Ashʿarism or Muʿtazilism, and both schools are deviant.

According to the example that I used earlier, the Imāms ﷺ are the specialists and the experts of the Qurʾān who speak based on knowledge that comes from emanation or at least from a special kind of teaching. Imām ʿAlī ﷺ tells Kumayl b. Ziyād, "Knowledge charged at them with the reality of insight and they had direct contact with the spirit of certainty. They found easy what the indulgent found difficult, and they found comfort in what the ignorant found lonesome." In another sermon in *Nahj al-Balāgha*, Imām ʿAlī ﷺ describes Ahl al-Bayt ﷺ as follows: "They are entrusted with Allah's secret. They are the safe haven of His command and the reference of His ruling. They are the caves of His books, and the mountains of His religion. Through them, Allah straightened Islam's back and calmed its quaking limbs ... No one in this *ummah* can be compared to Muḥammad's family, and they cannot be equated to the people who are forever beholden to them. They are the basis of religion and the pillar of certainty. The extremists go back to them, and those who fell short catch up to them. They have the particular right of guardianship, and the bequest and inheritance are among them." In another sermon, Imām ʿAlī ﷺ says, "Through us you were guided in the darkness and reached elevated heights. Through us you saw the dawn after the darkest night. Deaf be the ears that do not heed the call."

In sermon 147, Imām ʿAlī ﷺ says, "You will not uphold the pledge of the Book until you know those who broke the pledge, and you will not hold fast to the Book until you know those who abandoned it. Seek that knowledge with those who have it: they are the life of knowledge and the death of ignorance. Their judgment tells you about their knowledge, their silence tells you about their speech (or in sermon 237 "the wisdom of their speech"), and their exterior tells you about their interior. They never contradict religion or have differences about it. Religion among them is a truthful witness and a silent party that yet speaks." The sentence "They never contradict religion" indicates their infallibility, and the sentence stating that they do not have "differences about it" indicates their scholarly position. Both conditions are necessary in the divine specialist. In sermon 239, Imām ʿAlī ﷺ says, "they are the life of knowledge and the death of ignorance. Their forbearance (*ḥilm*) (in sermon 147 "their judgment") tells you about their knowledge, their silence tells you about their speech. They never contradict the Truth [i.e. infallibility] or have differences about it [this is a reference to correct and pure knowledge]. They are the pillars of Islam, and the means of holding fast. Through them, the Truth returned to its course and falsehood was ousted from its position, with its tongue cut off. They understood religion through their intellects with awareness and care, not through hearing and narration. The narrators of knowledge are many, but those who understand it are few."

In sermon 147, Imām ʿAlī ﷺ also says, "There will come upon you a time after me when nothing is more hidden than the Truth and nothing is more apparent than falsehood ... At that time, the Book and its people will be exiled outcasts and two companions on the same road. Not one person will give them refuge. The Book and its people will be among the people but not among them, and with them but not with them."